P9-DCJ-247

ARKANSAS STATE LIBRARY
Document Division
Little Rock, Arkansas 72

Property of
Mrs. Library Commission
Little Rock, Arkansas

PRIZE-WINNING AMERICAN DRAMA

A Bibliographical & Descriptive Guide

by

JANE F. BONIN

The Scarecrow Press, Inc.
Metuchen, N. J.   1973

Library of Congress Cataloging in Publication Data

Bonin, Jane F
    Prize-winning American drama: a bibliographical and
descriptive guide.

    1. American drama—20th century—History and
criticism. 2. American drama—Stories, plots, etc.
3. Literary prizes. I. Title.
PS351.B6   812'.5'09   73-3111
ISBN 0-8108-0607-X

Copyright 1973 by Jane F. Bonin

For Bill, Knowles, and William with affection

TABLE OF CONTENTS

Page

vi

vii

INTRODUCTION

The plays considered in this descriptive bibliography are winners of one or more of the following prizes for American drama: The Pulitzer Prize, The Critics' Circle Award, The Antoinette Perry Award (the Tony), The Village Voice Off-Broadway Award (the Obie), and The Players' Workshop Award. The study, which covers fifty-six years of the American theatre, begins in 1917 with Jessie Lynch Williams' Why Marry? (the first Pulitzer Prize winner), and continues through the 1970-71 season. The assumption underlying this collection is that familiarity with the materials here assembled will provide the reader with an important key, not only to American dramatic literature but to American culture as well.

One might argue that a study of only prize-winners leaves out some plays now considered classics in American literature and includes some which have now fallen into the oblivion they deserved in the beginning. Such is inevitably the case. The prize-givers, equipped with the luxury of hind-sight, would certainly make some adjustments. The Pulitzer Committee, for example, must wince when they remember that they passed up The Glass Menagerie for Harvey, or The Children's Hour for The Old Maid. Furthermore, if history should preserve only these plays, future students of American culture would not know Desire Under the Elms, Mourning Becomes Electra or The Little Foxes, to mention three which are now routinely anthologized. These problems are, unfortunately, endemic to the nature of prize-giving. The prizes given the plays of Aeschylus, Sophocles and Euripides, however, offer some sort of defense for accepting prize-giving as one means of calling attention to merit, even though we have undoubtedly missed some beautiful Greek plays which were not preserved because they lost the competition.

Obviously, with respect for all qualifications, if an historian knew only the works included here, he would have before him an impressive body of plays. He would know Death of a Salesman, Long Day's Journey Into Night, The

Glass Menagerie, Streetcar Named Desire. He would, in
fact, know four plays by O'Neill, three by Maxwell Anderson,
five by Tennessee Williams, four by Arthur Miller, three by
Robert E. Sherwood, two by Thornton Wilder, two by Lillian
Hellman, two by Edward Albee. Only the work of Clifford
Odets among our most significant playwrights would be lost
to him. In short, he would have access to most of the
plays that most critics agree are the important ones in
American dramatic literature.

He would also be in possession of some bad plays,
but these he would no doubt count as blessings, for bad
art is also useful in understanding a civilization. (To return to the Greeks--how much would we give to have even
the worst play submitted in any season?) A collection of
America's prize-winning drama, it seems to me, is indeed
a rich lode for the student of American life. One might,
for example, consider this body of plays an index to popular culture in the United States from about World War I to
the present. Most of the plays were commercial successes,
and many were exceptionally popular. They should, then,
reflect mainstream-American tastes. One could argue that
theatre-goers in New York City are not average Americans,
but the fact that many of these plays have been made into
motion pictures, have been performed on tours around the
country and have found their way into the repertoires of
provincial and amateur theatres suggests their broad appeal.

One might also look at these plays as a reflection
of the American value structure--a popular history of American ideas. Plays in general and prize-winning plays in
particular are a faithful barometer of a society's basic
assumptions and values. If a dramatist wants to survive,
he must make his appeal to an audience rather than to an
individual. He must serve a community of play-goers. If
his plays are peripheral to the concerns of the many or are
morally unintelligible to them, they will probably fail. Con-
versely, plays with general appeal reflect fundamental attitudes. Thus, fifty-six years worth of prize-winning plays
--which in the main constitutes the history of American
prize-giving for drama--should certainly reveal certain pat-
terns of assumptions, and, because our era is one of rapid
social change, certain shifts in moral postures and ethical
standards. They should, in other words, reaffirm or
challenge the premises upon which our culture rests.

Because we are a nation of prize-givers, the awards
chosen for study here do not include every award given each

season; but they are, I think, a representative group. The Pulitzer Prize, for example, is the most prestigious and conservative of the group. Its jurors have often been criticized for their failure to make an award to a play of artistic merit if it does not reflect the "American Spirit" as they conceive it (or wish it) to be. The Circle Award, not as conservative as the Pulitzer Prize but still solidly mainstream, was established by the New York drama critics in the mid-30's to rectify what they thought were errors in critical judgment or simple timidity on the part of the Pulitzer jurors. Least prestigious among serious critics is the Tony Award, the theatrical counterpart of the Oscar. According to Robert Brustein, the sole critical criterion of the Tony jurors is success at the box-office. Commercial success is, of course, one valuable index to mainstream American plays. The Obie Award, which usually goes to plays exhibiting innovative techniques and a more skeptical view of American life, provides a balance for the three more conservative awards and gives some indication of the ferment in the less traditional wing of the theatre. Finally, I have included the Players' Workshop Awards as an example of the kinds of prize winners chosen in serious provincial theatre. Taken altogether, the winners of these five awards should give a broad sample of the American plays which are respected and admired.

The organization of this descriptive bibliography is, I hope, a simple one. The bibliography is arranged by years (although the plays are indexed alphabetically), and each prize-winning play is described. These descriptions are probably the main contribution of this book. Following a summary of the play's action is a brief theatre history and a short, representative bibliography of contemporary reviews and standard criticism. These bibliographies make no claim to completeness; they are, in fact, highly selective and are intended to direct the reader to some useful discussions of the play. One who wishes to make an exhaustive study of a play or playwright should consider this study a starting place. These representative critical bibliographies should, however, be of some use to scholars who wish to see quickly which prize-winning American plays have, as yet, received only scant attention.

I must here acknowledge my great debt to Paul T. Nolan, without whose initial suggestion and constant encouragement this study would not have been possible. I am also indebted to Margaret Simpson, who typed the manuscript, and to Ruth Lefkovits, Louise Fisher and Diane

Moore, research librarians, who patiently ordered the reams of material used in the making of this book.

When Joseph Pulitzer left a portion of his fortune for the establishment of the Pulitzer Prize for Drama, he made possible the first significant award for American playwrights. During the 1917-1918 season the first Pulitzer Prize went to Jesse Lynch Williams for his play Why Marry? The play, remarkably sophisticated for the period, defeated The Copperhead, A Tailor Made Man, Seventeen, and The Country Cousin.

WHY MARRY?

Characters:

Jean	John
Rex	Uncle Everette
Lucy	Uncle Theodore
Helen	Ernest

Act I:

John, a wealthy businessman, has gathered his family to help him force his sister Jean to marry Rex, a rich man she does not love, and to keep his other sister, Helen, from marrying Ernest, a brilliant but penniless colleague she adores. Jean gives in, but Helen, an emancipated woman of twenty-nine, is not so easily intimidated. After Uncle Everette, a judge, and Uncle Theodore, a clergyman, arrive, Helen announces that she has no intention of marrying Ernest, who can ill afford a wife. His career in science matters more to her than marriage. The bewildered family now hopes that Ernest will propose, which he does. Although Helen is overjoyed at his profession of love, she insists they will never marry.

Act II:

After Ernest exhibits all the signs of the conventional

lover, John returns to his original position and refuses to
give his consent. Lucy, John's wife, revolted by his arro-
gance, timidly asks for a divorce, but John will not hear of
it. When Rex reluctantly asks for Jean's hand, John gives
permission with ill-concealed delight, but Jean, emboldened
by Helen's ability to control her destiny, tells Rex she cannot marry him because she loves a poor law student. Then
Helen announces to Ernest and her horrified family that
while her conscience will not permit her to marry Ernest,
she intends to become his mistress.

Act III:

John finally bullies the helpless Jean into accepting
Rex; later, however, she is saved from a loveless match
when Uncle Theodore refuses to perform the ceremony.
Uncle Everette then asks Helen and Ernest if they consider
themselves married in the sight of God. When they say
they do, he quickly proclaims, by the authority vested in
him as a judge, that they are husband and wife. At first
they are annoyed by the trick, but then decide to accept
the situation philosophically.

Theatre History and Popular Response:

Why Marry?, adapted from Williams' 1914 novel
And So They Were Married, opened in New York at the
Astor Theatre, December 25, 1917, and ran for 120 performances. The reviews were mixed, some critics complaining that the play was tedious and others describing it
as "clever," "amusing," and even "brilliant." Several
hailed Williams as the American Shaw and the play as a
contribution to the drama of ideas in America, a "comedy
with brains behind it." For some representative reviews,
see Dial, January 16, 1915, p. 48; Nation, December 24,
1914, p. 755; New Republic, December 5, 1914, p. 28; and
North American Review, February, 1918, pp. 278-281.

Critical Reputation:

Williams (1871-1929) is now remembered by drama
historians for this single play. For most of his life, however, he was associated with various aspects of literature.
A graduate of Princeton University, from which he received
the Litt. D. in 1919, Williams spent his life as a newspaper

reporter, short story writer, and novelist. His first play,
The Stolen Story, (1906), based on his newspaper experiences,
was produced more than two hundred times on the New York
stage and elsewhere around the country. The biographical
sketch in Kunitz and Haycraft's Twentieth Century Authors,
1942, is the fullest account of the man's life. Arthur Hobson Quinn's History of American Drama, 1927 (pp. 68-74),
contains an account of his work as a dramatist. It also
contains a brief discussion of Why Marry? as does Thomas
Dickinson's Playwrights of the New American Theatre, 1924
(pp. 223-237). The only recent essay dealing with the play
is Jane F. Bonin's "The First Pulitzer Prize for Drama,"
Vision, LXI (April 14, 1968), 12-13.

The Theatre Season of

1918-1919

        The Pulitzer Prize Committee gave no award this
season. Lightnin', by Winchell Smith and Frank Bacon,
was a success that ran for 1,291 performances, but according to John Toohey (A History of the Pulitzer Prize
Plays, 1967), the judges apparently did not want to give
"their shiny new award to a drunken old rascal, lovable or
not." Other plays running that season were: Three Wise
Fools, A Little Journey, and East Is West.

The Theatre Season of

1919-1920

Eugene O'Neill's play Beyond the Horizon won the second Pulitzer Prize for Drama, the only prize given during this season. The Pulitzer Prize was at this time still relatively unknown; in fact, O'Neill claimed he had never heard of it, but added that he was happy enough to take the thousand dollars. Other contenders for the prize were: The Famous Mrs. Fair, Adam and Eve, Clarence, and Declasse.

BEYOND THE HORIZON

Characters:

James Mayo	Ruth Atkins
Kate Mayo	Mrs. Atkins
Captain Dick Scott	Mary
Andrew Mayo	Ben
Robert Mayo	Dr. Fawcett

Act I:

When Robert Mayo discovers that Ruth, his brother Andrew's sweetheart, really loves him, he gives up his plans to go to sea. Andrew, a capable, stolid boy who loves farming, ships out in Robert's place; Robert, the dreamer, marries Ruth and takes over the family farm.

Act II:

Three years later, Robert and Ruth await Andrew's return. Robert has seriously mismanaged the farm and hopes his brother will set things right; Ruth, miserable with Robert, fancies Andrew still loves her. Andrew intends, however, to seek his fortune in the Argentine. The sea has cured him of his love for Ruth and given him instead a severe case of wanderlust.

4

Act III:

   When Andrew returns five years later, having lost
all his money in speculation, he finds the farm in complete
disorder and Robert dying of tuberculosis. After making
Andrew promise to marry Ruth, Robert dies, happy to end
his cramped and misspent life. Ruth, still a young woman
but broken and incapable of any emotion, knows the future
holds no happiness for her. On this dismal note, the play
ends.

Theatre History and Popular Response:

   Eugene O'Neill had some modest success with his
one-act plays staged by the Provincetown Players in Greenwich Village, but he was thirty-one years old before he saw
his first play produced on Broadway. Beyond the Horizon,
which opened on February 3, 1920, was a makeshift production with cheap sets, a cast recruited from other plays, and
performances scheduled only on weekday afternoons at the
Morosco Theatre. In spite of this inauspicious beginning,
the critics were impressed, and the play ran for the rest of
the season, 110 more performances. Although reviewers
commented on the occasional clumsiness of the play, almost
all agreed that Beyond the Horizon was a work of unusual
force and eloquence, "a significant and memorable tragedy."
For representative reviews, see: Independent, March 13,
1920, p. 382; Literary Digest, February 28, 1920, p. 33;
Nation, February 21, 1920, pp. 241-242; Theatre Arts, October 1920, pp. 286-289.

Critical Reputation:

   Eugene O'Neill (1899-1952), America's most celebrated
dramatist, recipient of four Pulitzer Prizes and the Critic's
Circle Award, became established as a major dramatist with
Beyond the Horizon. Prior to that time, he held odd jobs,
studied playwrighting at the famous 47 Workshop at Harvard,
and worked with the Provincetown Players. O'Neill, a prolific writer and a relentless innovator and experimentalist,
rose quickly to international prominence, winning the Nobel
Prize for Literature in 1936. For further information on
O'Neill's life, see The Tempering of Eugene O'Neill, 1962,
by Doris Alexander, and O'Neill, 1962, by Barbara and
Arthur Gelb, the definitive biography. An earlier but still

useful work is Barrett H. Clark's Eugene O'Neill: The Man and His Plays, 1947.

Criticism pertaining to O'Neill's work is by now a formidable mass of material. There are, however, four bibliographies. The most complete of these is Jordan Y. Miller's Eugene O'Neill and the American Critics: A Summary and Bibliographical Checklist, 1962. The others are: O'Neill and His Plays: Four Decades of Criticism, ed. by Oscar Cargill, N. B. Fagin, and W. J. Fisher, 1961; A Bibliography of the Works of Eugene O'Neill, 1931, by Ralph Sanborn and Barrett H. Clark; and Jackson Bryer's "Forty Years of O'Neill Criticism: A Selected Bibliography," Modern Drama, IV (1961), 196-216.

Literally dozens of books containing critical and interpretative material on O'Neill's plays are available. Some fairly recent ones are: Doris Falk's Eugene O'Neill and The Tragic Tension, 1958; Frederick I. Carpenter's Eugene O'Neill, 1964; John Gassner's Eugene O'Neill, 1965; and John H. Raleigh's The Plays of Eugene O'Neill, 1965.

While Beyond the Horizon has not received as much critical attention as many of O'Neill's later plays, it is a landmark in the history of American drama and receives consideration in the standard drama histories. For further critical comment, see the major studies of O'Neill's art listed above. See also the following scholarly articles: R. A. Dave's "Have We Lost the Tragic Sense? Eugene O'Neill's Beyond the Horizon: A Study," Literary Criticism (University of Mysore, India), VI (1965), 26-35; and Emil Roy's "Tragic Tension in Beyond the Horizon," Ball State University Forum, VIII (1967), 74-79.

The Theatre Season of

1920-1921

The Pulitzer Prize for the season of 1920-1921 went
to Zona Gale's comedy Miss Lulu Bett, which won over The
First Year, The Emperor Jones, The Bad Man, and Nice
People.

MISS LULU BETT

Characters:

Dwight Deacon   Lulu Bett
Ina Deacon   Mrs. Bett
Monona Deacon   Bobby Larkin
Diane Deacon   Mr. Cornish
Ninian Deacon

Act I:

Miss Lulu Bett, a maiden lady of 34, has for fifteen
years been an unpaid servant in the household of her brother-
in-law Dwight Deacon and her sister Ina. The Deacons and
their spoiled daughters grudgingly admire her efficiency in
the kitchen, but do not recognize her other fine qualities.
When Dwight's brother Ninian arrives from Oregon, he and
Lulu become fast friends. When Ninian, as a joke, gets
Lulu to recite the marriage vows with him, Dwight, a judge,
declares that they are legally married. Ninian persuades
Lulu to let the marriage stand, and they depart on their
wedding trip.

Act II:

A week later, Lulu returns without Ninian, who had
confessed on the honeymoon that he was once married to
another woman, long departed and now presumed dead. Lulu,
unwilling to live with him until the legality of their marriage

7

is established, resumes her position at the Deacon's.
Dwight, insisting that appearances must be maintained, instructs Lulu to tell people she separated from her husband
because they were incompatible.   Lulu wants to defy Dwight
and tell the truth to the neighbors, but Dwight, more concerned about the Deacon family's respectability than Lulu's
pride, threatens to have Ninian sent to prison as a bigamist
if she tells her story.

Act III:

      Lulu, no longer able to bear life with Dwight and Ina,
who now consider her a fallen woman, decides to leave
home.   At this point Ninian arrives with proof that his former wife is dead, and he and Lulu are happily reunited.

Theatre History and Popular Response:

      Miss Lulu Bett opened, oddly enough, at Sing Sing as
a premiere performance by David Belasco when he presented
the prison with the "Belasco Stage," a portable stage which
could be erected and dismantled with ease.   The following
night, December 27, 1920, the play opened on Broadway at
the Belmont Theatre and ran for 176 performances.   The
play, adapted from Miss Gale's best-selling novel of the
same name, was not an unqualified critical success.   Although some called it "delightful," and "thrilling," many
complained that the play was "dull and flabby," its construction rather "sleazy," and its story poorly adjusted to
the medium of the theatre.   Another storm of criticism was
unleashed when the author, in response to audience demands
for a happy ending, rewrote the last act.   In the original
version, Lulu is left alone when Ninian's wife turns up.   The
second version provides for the convenient disposal of the
first wife, leaving Lulu a respectable married woman.   Although critics accused Miss Gale of bowing down before the
public taste, the controversy increased the popularity of the
play; and, according to one critic, the months of solid book-
ing made it a contender for the Pulitzer Prize.   For representative reviews see: Collier's, January 29, 1921, p. 13;
The Literary Review, December 3, 1921, p. 221; The Nation, February 2, 1921, p. 189; The New Republic, January
12, 1921, pp. 204-205.

Critical Reputation:

    Miss Gale (1874-1938), a native of Wisconsin, re-
ceived the M.S. from the University of Wisconsin in 1899.
She began her career as a newspaper reporter, first for
various Milwaukee papers and then for the New York World.
A prolific writer, she is best remembered for her numerous
novels, short stories, and essays; her plays have received
little serious critical attention. For a good critical biography and assessment of her contribution to American letters,
see Harold P. Simonson's Zona Gale, 1962.

The Theatre Season of

1921-1922

The Pulitzer Prize this season went again to Eugene
O'Neill for his play Anna Christie. Also running were Dulcy,
Six-Cylinder Love, To The Ladies, The Hero, and another
O'Neill play, The Hairy Ape.

ANNA CHRISTIE

Characters:

Johnny-the-Priest	Marty Owen
Two Longshoremen	Anna Christopherson
A Postman	Three Men of a steamer's crew
Larry	Mat Burke
Chris Christopherson	Johnson

Act I:

In Johnny-the-Priest's saloon, Chris Christopherson,
an old Swedish sailor, now captain of a coal barge, is reunited with his daughter Anna, whom he has not seen since
she was a child. Chris, not realizing that Anna is a prostitute, worries because she looks so worn and sick. Finally,
he convinces the reluctant girl to live on the barge until she
regains her health.

Act II:

After ten days, Anna seems a new person. Her
health is restored, and proximity to the sea has made her
feel clean again. When the coal barge picks up some ship-
wrecked sailors, she meets Mat Burke, a rugged, passionate
Irishman. He falls in love with Anna at first sight, declaring
ironically that she is the first "dacent" girl he has ever
known.

Act III:

  Chris, who has an obsessive fear of Anna's marrying
a sailor, watches with dismay as the romance progresses
and tries, without success, to break it up. Anna loves Mat,
but when he proposes, she declares they can never marry.
She intended to keep her past a secret, but when Mat bullies
her to explain her refusal, she blurts out the truth. Chris
and Mat, unable to face her after this revelation, leave the
barge for an epic drunk.

Act IV:

  Two days later Mat returns and makes Anna swear
on a crucifix that she never loved any other man but him.
After they make plans to be married, Mat and Chris reveal
that they have signed aboard a freighter and must ship out
soon. Mat and Anna hope they can be happy together, but
Chris, still a fatalist, thinks the "ole devil sea" controls the
destiny of them all.

Theatre History and Popular Response:

  The first version of the play that was to become
Anna Christie was called Chris Christopherson and concerned
a proper young lady whose father refused to let her marry a
sailor. When the play failed, O'Neill rewrote it, changing
Anna from an innocent girl to a fading prostitute. The new
play, which opened at the Vanderbilt Theatre on November 2,
1921, was well received by critics and subsequently ran for
177 performances. Most reviewers were gripped by the un-
compromising realism--the sheer ugliness--of the play. Although nearly all recognized the dramatic power of Anna
Christie, several were annoyed at the ending, which asks the
audience to believe that a prostitute and a puritanical Irish
Catholic can live happily ever after. O'Neill steadily maintained, however, that the play was not sentimentalized but
ended ambiguously. For representative reviews see: Current Opinion, January, 1922, pp. 57-66; Dial, December,
1921, pp. 724-725; Independent, December 3, 1921, p. 326;
Theatre Arts, January, 1922, p. 70; Literary Digest, May
26, 1923, pp. 28-29.

Critical Reputation:

    For a general introduction to Eugene O'Neill's biography, bibliography, and critical reputation, see the entry for 1919-1920. For discussions of <u>Anna Christie</u> consult the critical studies of O'Neill's work listed above, most of which devote a few pages to this play. For a perceptive scholarly article on <u>Anna Christie</u>, see John J. McAleer's "Christ Symbolism in <u>Anna Christie</u>," <u>Modern Drama</u>, IV (1962), 389-396. Also of interest is Gary A. Vena's "The Role of the Prostitute in the Plays of Eugene O'Neill," <u>Drama Critique</u>, X (1967), 129-137, and XI (1968), 9-14, 82-88.

The Theatre Season of

1922-1923

The Pulitzer Prize for this season was awarded to
Icebound, by Owen Davis, selected over The Adding Machine,
You and I, The Torchbearers, The Fool, and Why Not?

ICEBOUND

Characters:

Henry Jordan	Doctor Curtis
Emma	Jane Crosby
Nettie	Judge Bradford
Sadie Fellows	Ben Jordan
Orin	Hannah
Ella Jordan	Jim Jay

Act I:

When the grim old matriarch of the Jordan clan dies,
her avaricious children are astonished to discover that she
has left the bulk of her estate to Jane Crosby, a cousin.
Jane immediately takes command of the farm and sets out to
reform Ben, Mother Jordan's youngest son, a fugitive from
justice released in her custody until his trial.

Act II:

After two months, Jane has turned Ben into a hard-
working farmer. He grumbles occasionally about his "slav-
ery," but since Jane has arranged to have the criminal
charges against him dropped, he can hardly complain for
long. Jane, secretly in love with Ben, longs for his complete rehabilitation, but when he falls momentarily under the
spell of his pretty but shallow cousin, Nettie, Jane despairs
of winning his affection.

13

Act III:

Jane renounces her inheritance and prepares to turn the farm over to Ben, who immediately realizes that he loves only her. He begs her to stay, and she confesses her love; as the curtain falls, they make plans to be married.

Theatre History and Popular Response:

Owen Davis wrote literally hundreds of plays during his lifetime, most of them popular melodramas. Icebound, one of his rare attempts at a serious play, opened at the Sam H. Harris Theatre on February 10, 1923, and closed 171 performances later. In spite of its sluggish action, trite love theme, and sentimental ending, many critics were impressed with Icebound as a slice of New England life and praised Davis's handling of the grimly American characterizations, dialogue, and tone. For representative reviews see: Current Opinion, May, 1923, pp. 574-579; Literary Review, September 15, 1923, p. 38; Theatre Magazine, April, 1923, p. 20.

Critical Response:

Owen Davis (1894-1956), one of America's prolific playwrights, was a native of Portland, Maine, and studied civil engineering at the University of Tennessee and Harvard. The lure of the theatre proved strong, however, and he turned to acting and cranking out commercially successful melodramas, plays like Nellie: The Beautiful Cloak Model and Chinatown Charlie. In addition to writing plays, he also dramatized serious works, such as Ethan Frome and The Great Gatsby, for the motion picture theatre. There is no full-length study of Davis's almost legendary place in the history of the American theatre, but the standard drama histories devote space to him. See Arthur Hobson Quinn's A History of The American Drama, 1927, pp. 217-220, and Burns Mantle's chapter "Owen Davis" in Contemporary American Playwrights, 1938. For a brief account of Davis's versatility, see Montrose J. Moses' "Owen Davis: The Infallible Playwright Whose Gamut Extends from the Thriller to a Pulitzer Prize Play," Theatre Guild Magazine, VIII (1930), 42-44. The sketch in Kunitz and Haycraft's Twentieth Century Authors, 1942, contains further details of his life. To date, Icebound has received no scholarly interest.

The Theatre Season of

1923-1924

The Pulitzer Prize was awarded this season to Hatcher Hughes' melodrama Hell Bent fer Heaven. The Show-Off, a comedy by George Kelly, had first been selected by the Pulitzer judges, but the advisory board overruled their verdict and gave the prize to Hughes. Also running were The Changelings, Tarnish, and Sun-Up.

HELL BENT FER HEAVEN

Characters:

David Hunt   Matt Hunt
Meg Hunt   Aunt Lowry
Sid Hunt   Jude Lowry
Rufe Pryor

Act I:

When Sid Hunt returns to his Carolina mountain home after World War I, everyone rejoices except Rufe Pryor. Rufe, considered a religious maniac even in the Bible Belt, has been a handyman for the Hunts in Sid's absence, but with Sid's return, Rufe's place is threatened. To add to Rufe's frustration, Sid resumes courting Jude Lowry, the girl Rufe vainly loves. Rufe skillfully reactivates an ancient family feud between the Hunts and the Lowrys by inciting Andy Lowry, Jude's brother and Sid's best friend, to quarrel with Sid.

Act II:

When Andy begins talking wildly about settling the old score, Sid, aware that Andy is drunk, reacts with amusement. When Andy sobers up and apologizes, Sid decides to see him home, but Rufe tells Andy that Sid means to kill him once they get into the mountains. Later, when Sid's

15

riderless horse comes back to the house, the Hunts, con-
cluding that Andy has made good his threats, arm themselves and set out in a driving storm to avenge the murder.
Meanwhile, Sid returns and realizing that Rufe is responsible
for the mischief, goes out to send a warning to the Lowrys.

Act III:

When the men of the Hunt clan return with Andy in
tow, they are tempted to shoot him, but loathe to set the
old vendetta going again, they hesitate. Rufe, now desperate,
convinced he is the instrument of the Lord, dynamites a dam,
hoping that the rising waters will sweep Sid away. Miraculously, Sid escapes, Rufe's villainy is exposed, and the families patch up the quarrel.

Theatre History and Popular Response:

This play, like Beyond the Horizon, was first produced with only matinee performances scheduled. It opened
at the Klaw Theatre on January 4, 1924, but was later
moved to the Frazee Theatre for a regular engagement and
ran for 122 performances. The Pulitzer Prize was a post-
humous award, however, for Hell Bent fer Heaven closed
the night before the announcement was made. The notices
were, for the most part, favorable, with reviewers calling
the play "extraordinary," "rich," "poetic," and "intensely
interesting." A few complained about the play's structure,
and one, Carl Van Doren, was irritated because Rufe does
not get his just deserts in the denouement. The consensus
was, however, that Hell Bent was a "darned good melodrama." For representative reviews, see The Literary
Review, May 17, 1924, p. 754; Nation, January 16, 1924,
p. 68; Outlook, May 28, 1924, p. 158.

Critical Reputation:

Hughes (1884-1945), born in Polkville, North Carolina, received his B.A. from the University of North Carolina and his M.A. at Columbia; he later taught English and
playwriting at both schools. Hell Bent reflects his abiding
interest in the customs and folklore of his native state, but
in addition to folk plays Hughes also tried his hand at farce
and at family comedy. He achieved a modest success with
the play Wake Up, Jonathan (1928) which he wrote in collab-

oration with Elmer Rice. For a fuller account of his career,
see Kunitz and Haycraft's sketch in Twentieth Century Authors, 1942. See also Grace Leake's "Southern Personali-
ties: Hatcher Hughes, Dramatist, " Holland's, February,
1937, p. 12. Otherwise, Hughes receives only passing
comments in the standard histories of American drama and
Hell Bent has not aroused any scholarly interest.

The Theatre Season of

1924-1925

Still the only prize of national importance, the Pulitzer went this year to Sidney Howard's They Knew What They Wanted. Other plays which were given serious attention include What Price Glory?, a runner-up for the Pulitzer Prize, Desire Under the Elms, Processional, Minick, The Youngest, and Dancing Mothers.

THEY KNEW WHAT THEY WANTED

Characters:

Amy	The R. F. D.
Tony	Ah Gee
Joe	Two Italian Farmhands
Father McKee	Italian Wedding Guests
The Doctor	

Act I:

Tony Patucci, a prosperous 60-year-old California winegrower of Italian descent, nervously awaits the arrival of his bride, a waitress from San Francisco. Because they have never met--their courtship was conducted entirely by mail--Tony is uneasy, especially since he sent Amy a picture of his handsome young assistant Joe rather than one of himself. In his agitation, Tony drinks too much, then sets off to meet Amy's train. Meanwhile, Amy appears, furious because no one met her at the station. When she sees Joe, she naturally assumes he is the bridegroom. Before he can explain, Tony is brought in badly injured from an automobile accident. When Amy realizes that her prospective husband is an old man with two broken legs, she considers returning to the city, but decides instead to go through with the marriage.

Act II:

     Later that day the wedding takes place, followed by a real Italian festival, complete with singing, dancing, and much wine drinking. Amy, still rather sullen, declares that she will care for Tony herself instead of hiring a nurse. Tony, delirious with joy, is put to bed, leaving Amy to reveal her unhappiness to Joe, who, sensing his advantage, seduces her.

Act III:

     Three months later, after Amy has learned to love Tony, she discovers that she is pregnant as the result of her one encounter with Joe. Joe rather reluctantly offers to take her away with him, but Amy will not leave until she has explained to Tony that she loves him and not Joe. Tony reacts with fury but then decides Amy should stay. Tony, with his great capacity for love, wants a large family, and furthermore, he knows that Amy could never be happy with Joe.

Theatre History and Popular Response:

     They Knew What They Wanted, which opened at the Garrick Theatre on November 24, 1924, for a lengthy run of 414 performances, was warmly received by critics and public alike. The reviewers called it "a peach of a play," a "mature and sophisticated comedy," "a colorful piece cut from the genuine fabric of American life." Although the reviewers were enthusiastic, some later said What Price Glory? should have received the prize. Indeed, Howard himself (Stage Magazine, February, 1935) called What Price Glory? "the great American play." For representative reviews see: Current Opinion, February, 1925, p. 188; Independent, January 10, 1925, p. 51; Nation, December 10, 1924, pp. 662-663; Theatre Arts, February, 1925, p. 77.

Critical Reputation:

     Sidney Howard (1891-1939), born in Oakland, California, was graduated from the University of California at Berkeley in 1915 and went on to study playwriting with George Pierce Baker at Harvard. He wrote feature articles for several well-known magazines and was literary editor of

one, but he is best remembered as one of the first major
writers of social drama in America. His death at 44, the
result of a tractor accident, cut short his promising career.
Neither Howard nor his prize-winning play has become a
standard part of serious American literary scholarship; both
have, however, received some attention. Kunitz and Haycraft's Twentieth Century Authors, 1942, contains a sketch
of his life. Most standard histories of drama in America
devote space to Howard and his work: see for example,
Eleanor Flexner's chapter "Sidney Howard," in American
Playwrights, 1918-1938; and Burns Mantle's appraisal in
American Playwrights of Today, 1938. Two articles which
discuss his plays are Barrett H. Clark's "Sidney Howard:
A Critical Appraisal of an Intensely Serious Playwright,"
Theatre Guild Magazine, VIII (1930), 21-22, 25-26; and
Walter J. Meserve's "Sidney Howard and the Social Drama
of the Twenties," Modern Drama, VI (1963), 256-266. For
discussions of They Knew What They Wanted, consult Joseph
Wood Krutch's American Drama Since 1918, rev. ed., 1957,
pp. 26-72; and George Jean Nathan's Theatre Book of the
Year, 1948-9, pp. 286-295.

The Theatre Season of

1925-1926

The Pulitzer Prize this season went to <u>Craig's Wife</u>
by George Kelly. The play, Kelly's third Broadway success
in three years, defeated <u>The Wisdom Tooth</u>, <u>The Enemy</u>,
<u>Outside Looking In</u>, <u>The Butter and Egg Man</u>, <u>The Great
God Brown</u> and <u>Lucky Sam McCarver</u>.

CRAIG'S WIFE

Characters:

Miss Austen	Mrs. Frazier
Mrs. Harold	Billy Birkmire
Mazie	Joseph Catelle
Mrs. Craig	Harry
Ethel Landreth	Eugene Fredericks
Walter Craig	

Act I:

Walter Craig, his wife Harriet, and his Aunt Austen
live together in a house which, because of Harriet's fanatical
sense of order, is more an antiseptic museum than a home.
Miss Austen, realizing that Harriet is a shallow and vicious
woman, tries to tell her nephew that his wife loves only her
furniture, but Walter, a generous and rather romantic man,
cannot see the truth. One afternoon Walter learns that his
friend, Fergus Passmore, with whom he had played cards the
previous evening, has been found dead, together with his
wife.

Act II:

When two detectives come to question Walter, Harriet,
fearing a scandal, urges her astonished husband to lie about
his visit to the Passmore home. When Walter suddenly re-

21

alizes that Aunt Austen was right about Harriet, that she
does indeed care only for appearances, he defiantly lights a
cigarette in the immaculate living room and then smashes
one of Harriet's prized ornaments.

Act III:

By the following morning, the police have solved the
mystery of the Passmore death. Harriet assumes the quarrel with Walter is over, but Walter, having glimpsed Harriet's true nature, is so revolted that he moves out, as do
Miss Austen and the housekeeper whom Harriet has tormented
daily. As the play ends, Harriet is left alone in the great
house, wandering desolately from room to room.

Theatre History and Popular Response:

Craig's Wife opened at the Morosco Theatre on October 12, 1925, and ran for 289 performances. The notices
were, for the most part, favorable; one reviewer even called
it "one of the finest plays ever written by an American." A
few complained, however, that Kelly was given the prize only
because his play The Show-Off had been passed over two
seasons before. For representative reviews see: American
Mercury, December, 1925, pp. 504-5; Independent, November 21, 1925, p. 586; Nation, November 4, 1925, pp. 521-
522; New Republic, November 4, 1925, pp. 281-282.

Critical Reputation:

George Kelly (1887-   ) was born in Philadelphia into
a distinguished theatre family. (The "Virginia Judge" of
Vaudeville fame was his brother; Grace Kelly, now Princess
of Monaco, is his niece.) Privately educated, he never attended college, but began learning the theatre from childhood.
He played many juvenile roles, then went into Vaudeville
where he acted and wrote his own sketches. His three
Broadway successes in as many years suggested an exciting
career, but he was never able to repeat the successes of the
Twenties. For further information about his life and his
plays, see Kunitz and Haycraft, Twentieth Century Authors,
1942. Kelly has not been the subject of any serious, full-
length studies, but for general information, see Thomas
Dickinson's "Modern Domestic Comedy: George Kelly, " in
Playwrights of the New American Theatre, 1924; Montrose

Moses's discussion of Kelly in his book Dramas of Modern-
ism and Their Forerunners, 1941; Burns Mantle's "George
Kelly," in American Playwrights of Today, 1938; Kenneth
White's "George Kelly and Dramatic Device," Horn and
Hound, IV (April, 1931), 384-400; Arthur Willis' "The Kelly
Play," Modern Drama, VI (1963), 245-255. For specific
discussions of Craig's Wife see: W. L. Dusenbury's chapter, "Conflict between the Spiritual and the Material," in
Theme of Loneliness in Modern American Drama, 1960, pp.
155-178; and George Jean Nathan's Theatre Book of the Year,
1946-47, pp. 307-310.

The Theatre Season of

1926-1927

For this season, the Pulitzer, still the only prize of national significance, went to Paul Green's In Abraham's Bosom, an unorthodox selection. The play itself was not a box office success; yet it defeated such plays as The Silver Cord, Broadway, Saturday's Children, and The Road to Rome. Pulitzer juror Walter Prichard Eaton later explained that the play was selected because "it came up out of the soil of the South, and with a passionate sincerity tried to say something important about the Negro problem...."

IN ABRAHAM'S BOSOM

Characters:

Abraham McCranie	Douglass McCranie
Goldie McAllister	Eddie Williams
Muh Mack	Lanie Horton
Bud Gaskins	Neilly McNeill
Lije Hunneycutt	Colonel McCranie
Puny Avery	Lonnie McCranie

Scene I:

Abraham McCranie, a mulatto, the illegitimate son of Colonel McCranie, works as a laborer on his father's plantation but dreams of being a teacher and leader of the black man. When his white half-brother, Lonnie, taunts him, Abe strikes back and is savagely beaten by the Colonel.

Scene II:

When Abe marries and has a child, Colonel McCranie, to salve his conscience, promises Abe a small farm and an opportunity to teach the black children of the plantation.

24

Scene III:

Abe, frustrated at the indolence of the children at his school, beats one of the lazier boys and is dismissed from his post.

Scene IV:

Fifteen years later, now living in poverty in a Durham slum, Abe admits that his schemes for the betterment of the Negro have met with nothing but apathy. Furthermore, his son Douglass has been corrupted by life in the city.

Scene V:

After three years as a sharecropper on Lonnie's plantation, Abe is still struggling to get his school going again.

Scene VI:

Abe is beaten by some white men who fear that he preaches equality for the black man. Then Lonnie tells him that he is taking his land away from him. Mad with frustration and rage, Abe beats Lonnie to death.

Scene VII:

When Abe is overtaken by a lynch mob, he dies still preaching the black man's need for education.

Theatre History and Popular Response:

In Abraham's Bosom, staged by the Provincetown Players, opened at the Provincetown Theatre, December 30, 1926, and closed 123 performances later. Most of the critics conceded that the play contained moments of poetic power and authentic tragic feeling, but many complained that the play dragged and tended toward preachment. For representative reviews, see: Drama, February, 1927, p. 136; Literary Digest, May 28, 1927, pp. 27-8; New Republic, March 2, 1927, pp. 46-7; Theater Magazine, July, 1927, p. 18.

Critical Reputation:

Paul Green (1894-   ), born on a farm near Lillington,
North Carolina, worked in the cotton fields as a boy and received only scant formal education. Later, after earning his
tuition by playing semi-professional baseball, he attended the
University of North Carolina at Chapel Hill, where he studied
playwriting under Fred Koch. Although he has taught, written for Hollywood, and edited a literary quarterly, he now
devotes himself almost exclusively to outdoor or "symphonic"
drama. He is the author of The Lost Colony (1937), The
Founders (1957), The Confederacy (1958), and Stephen Foster
(1959)--all pageants that blend historical drama, music and
spectacle.

Green's work has attracted a modest amount of scholarly interest. There are, for example, two book-length
studies of the playwright and his plays: Barrett H. Clark's
Paul Green, 1928, and a more recent work, Agatha Adam's
Paul Green of Chapel Hill, 1951. He also receives attention
in the standard studies of American drama; see, for example,
Quinn's appraisal in A History of the American Drama, 1927,
pp. 243-246, and Burns Mantle's chapter "Paul Green," in
Contemporary American Playwrights, 1938. For discussions
of In Abraham's Bosom see A. C. Block's The Changing
World in Plays and Theatre, 1939, and Stark Young's Im-
mortal Shadows, 1948, 88-90.

The Theatre Season of

1927-1928

The Pulitzer Prize went this season to Eugene
O'Neill's massive play, Strange Interlude. The longest
play ever staged professionally in America, it ran to nine
acts, and featured an intermission for dinner. The play,
towering over its competition, handily defeated Coquette,
The Royal Family, Porgy, Paris Bound and Behold the
Bridegroom.

STRANGE INTERLUDE

Characters:

Charles Marsden	Sam Evans
Prof. Henry Leeds	Mrs. Amos Evans
Nina Leeds	Gordon Evans
Edmund Darrell	Madeline Arnold

Act I:

When Charles Marsden, a fussy bachelor, calls on
his friend Prof. Leeds, he learns that the old scholar's
daughter Nina has been bordering on a nervous collapse
since the wartime death of her fiance, Gordon. Charles,
secretly attracted to Nina himself, witnesses a scene in
which Nina blames her father because she refused, on moral
grounds, to become Gordon's mistress before he died. She
announces, to the consternation of both men, that she will
become a nurse in a hospital for wounded veterans.

Act II:

When Nina returns a year later for her father's funeral, accompanied by two friends, Dr. Edmund Darrell and
Sam Evans, Marsden still hopes she will show some interest
in him. After learning from Darrell that Nina has given

27

herself indiscriminately to one soldier after another in an
attempt to pay for withholding herself from Gordon, Marsden
agrees with the doctor that Nina should marry Evans, an innocent boy who would be a stabilizing influence.

Act III:

Nina attains a measure of serenity after she and Sam
marry and she becomes pregnant. Her happiness is cut
short, however, when Mrs. Evans tells her of the hereditary
insanity in the Evans family and persuades her to have an
abortion. Nina, who never revealed her pregnancy to Sam,
secretly vows to give him a child by another man.

Act IV:

When Nina aska Dr. Darrell to father her next child,
he agrees, masking his deep attraction for Nina behind a
pose of scientific detachment.

Act V:

Darrell and Nina fall desperately in love. Nina, now
carrying his child, wants to divorce Sam and marry her
lover. Darrell refuses. He has a bad conscience and
fears, moreover, that marriage will wreck his career. He
departs abruptly for Europe, leaving Nina with Sam, who is
blissfully happy and totally unaware of the complications.

Act VI:

Marsden's suspicions that Darrell and Nina were
lovers are confirmed when Darrell suddenly returns from
Europe. The doctor begs Nina to elope with him, but she
refuses, partly because of Sam and little Gordon, the baby,
and partly because she thrives on the adoration of all three
men.

Act VII:

Eleven years pass. Sam, now immensely wealthy,
never realizes that Gordon is not his son or that Nina and
Darrell are lovers. Darrell embittered by years of loving
Nina in secret and by seeing his son reared as Sam's,
senses that Nina finds him tedious now. She also resents
Sam's having the larger share of young Gordon's affection.

Act VIII:

> After ten years, Darrell has shaken off his emotional enslavement to Nina, who is now wholly preoccupied with trying to win Gordon's affection away from Madeline, his fiancee. Nina finally confesses to Marsden that Darrell has not only been her lover but is Gordon's father as well. Sam has a stroke before Nina is able to tell him too.

Act IX:

> Sam dies, never suspecting the truth. Gordon reveals that he has always intuited Nina's love for Darrell and suggests they marry. Darrell and Nina, however, no longer want each other. Nina decides to marry Marsden, hoping that with him she will find the peace she so desperately needs.

Theatre History and Popular Response:

> Strange Interlude, which opened at the John Golden Theatre on January 30, 1928, had a lengthy run of 426 performances and was such a tour de force that no critic could remain lukewarm in its presence. They tended, therefore, to write in superlatives. Some called it "the finest, the profoundest drama" of O'Neill's career, and "the greatest of American plays"; others fired great salvos of vituperation, labelling the play a "sordid mess," pompous, naive, and tasteless. For representative reviews, see: American Mercury, August, 1927, pp. 499-506; Nation, February 15, 1928, p. 192; New Republic, February 15, 1928, pp. 349-350; Theatre Arts, April, 1928, pp. 237-240.

Critical Reputation:

> For general information on O'Neill's biography and critical reputation, see the 1919-1920 entry. Strange Interlude itself has excited a good deal of critical interest, and nearly all of the general critical works bearing on the whole body of O'Neill's work contain discussions of this play. See also the following critical articles: Doris Alexander, "Strange Interlude and Schopenhauer," American Literature, XXV (May, 1953), 213-228; Roy Battenhouse, "Strange Interlude Restudied," Religion in Life, XV (Spring, 1946), 202-213; William Brashear, "O'Neill's Schopenhauer Interlude," Criti-

cism, VI (1964), 256-265; Kemp Malone, "The Diction of Strange Interlude," American Speech, VI (October, 1930), 19-28; Guy Montgomery, "Strange Interlude," University of California Chronicles, XXX (July, 1928), 364-368; Horace Shipp, "The X-Rays up to Nature," English Review, LII (March, 1931), 378-380; Stella Wynne, "The Strange Interlude," Overland, LXXXII (July, 1929), 220.   For a longer study of the impact of the play, see Harry Watson's The Historic Significance of Eugene O'Neill's Strange Interlude, 1928.

The Theatre Season of

1928-1929

Elmer Rice received the Pulitzer Prize this year for his play Street Scene. Ironically, many Broadway producers had been afraid to touch this play, which called for a teeming cast, an expensive realistic setting, and many special effects. Finally, Rice himself was forced to take over the direction of the play. The play was an immediate success and won an easy victory over its competition--Holiday, The Front Page, Gypsy, Machinal, and Gods of the Lightning.

STREET SCENE

Characters:

Abraham Kaplan	George Jones
Greta Florentino	Steve Sankey
Emma Jones	Agnes Cushing
Olga Olsen	Carl Olsen
Willie Maurrant	Shirley Kaplan
Anna Maurrant	Filippo Fiorentino
Daniel Buchannan	Alice Simpson
Frank Maurrant	Laura Hildebrand
Samuel Kaplan	A Music Student
Rose Maurrant	Marshall James Henry
Harry Easter	Fred Cullen
Mae Jones	An Old-Clothes Man
Dick McGann	An Interne
Vincent Jones	An Ambulance Driver
Dr. John Wilson	A Furniture Mover
Officer Harry Murphy	Two Nurse-Maids
A Milkman	Policemen
A Letter Carrier	Two Apartment-Hunters
An Ice-Man	Passers-by
Two College Girls	

<u>Act I:</u>

   In an ugly New York brownstone, the tenants--people
of many nationalities and degrees of poverty--distract themselves from the heat by following Anna Maurrant's love affair with the milkman, Steve Sankey. The gossip particularly
distresses Anna's daughter Rose, herself a person of more
than passing interest to the neighbors because of her affection for Sam Kaplan, the son of a radical Jew. The tenement dwellers also discuss the impending eviction of Mrs.
Hildebrand, watch the children who roller-skate by, and
await the arrival of Mrs. Buchannan's baby, expected momentarily.

<u>Act II:</u>

   When Anna's brutish husband, Frank, leaves for work,
she signals Sankey to come up to her apartment. Sam Kaplan sees Frank return and tries to prevent his entering the
building, but Frank, in a towering rage, bursts in, shoots
the lovers, and then escapes. Rose returns from an errand
just in time to see her mother taken away to the hospital.

<u>Act III:</u>

   Later that afternoon, Anna dies, the police capture
Frank, and Rose prepares to move away with her little
brother. Sam begs Rose to marry him, but Rose refuses,
telling him that people must belong only to themselves. As
Rose leaves, a pair of house-hunters come to look at the
Maurrant apartment, while the rest of the tenants resume
the lives they were leading before the tragedy.

<u>Theatre History and Popular Response:</u>

   <u>Street Scene</u> opened at The Playhouse on January 10,
1929, to good notices and had a long run of more than 600
performances. Most critics agreed that the play was vibrant,
engrossing, and strikingly original. One called it a "generous, juicy and enormously interesting slice of New York
life. " A dissenter called the play "an exhibition of pointless
realism. " For representative reviews see: <u>Nation,</u> January
30, 1929, p. 142; <u>New Republic,</u> January 30, <u>1929,</u> pp. 296-
298; <u>Outlook,</u> January 23, <u>1929,</u> p. 140; <u>Theatre Arts,</u>
March, <u>1929,</u> pp. 164-166.

Critical Reputation:

      Elmer Rice (1892-1967), was a native of New York,
born Elmer Reitzenstein. Educated in the New York public
schools and New York University, he became a lawyer but
gave up his practice to devote himself to playwriting. An
important figure in American drama, Rice wrote one of the
first expressionistic plays with an American background--
The Adding Machine (1923)--and was a pioneer in the use of
the now familiar "flashback" technique. He collaborated with
Hatcher Hughes, Dorothy Parker, and Phillip Barry and was
associated with Maxwell Anderson, Robert E. Sherwood,
Sidney Howard, and S. N. Behrman in the Playwrights'
Producing Company, a group formed for the purpose of fi-
nancing and producing the plays of its members. Rice, a
man of intense social concern, often wrote plays which mir-
rored his interest in liberal causes and social reform. For
a book-length study of Rice and his position in American
drama see Robert Hogan's The Independence of Elmer Rice,
1965. Most of the major studies of American drama contain discussions of his work. See John Gassner's The Theatre in Our Time, 1954; Jean Gould's Modern American Playwrights, 1966; Joseph Wood Krutch's American Drama Since
1918, 1939; Alan Lewis' American Plays and Playwrights of
the Contemporary Theatre, 1965; and Gerald Rabkin's Drama
and Commitment, 1964. Street Scene has received little
serious scholarly attention.

The Theatre Season of

1929-1930

As the decade of the Twenties came to an end, the Pulitzer Prize was still the only award of national importance for drama. It went this season to Marc Connelly's The Green Pastures, a play that towered over its competition-- The Criminal Code, The Last Mile, June Moon, Rebound and Hotel Universe. As Alexander Woollcott observed, the Pulitzer Prize needed The Green Pastures a good deal more than The Green Pastures needed the Pulitzer Prize.

THE GREEN PASTURES

Characters:

Mr. Deshee, the Preacher	First Mammy Angel
Myrtle	A Stout Angel
First Boy	A Slender Angel
Second Boy	Archangel
First Cook	Gabriel
A Voice	God
Second Cook	Choir Leader
First Man Angel	Custard Maker
Adam	Abraham
Eve	Isaac
Cain	Jacob
Cain's Girl	Moses
Zeba	Zipporah
Cain the Sixth	Aaron
Boy Gambler	A Candidate Magician
First Gambler	Pharaoh
Second Gambler	General
Voice in Shanty	Head Magician
Noah	First Wizard
Noah's Wife	Second Wizard
Shem	Joshua
First Woman	First Scout

Second Woman   Master of Ceremonies
Third Woman   King of Babylon
First Man   Prophet
Flatfoot   High Priest
Ham   Corporal
Japheth   Hezdrel
First Cleaner   Second Officer
Second Cleaner

Part I

Scene I:

In a Negro Sunday School class in South Louisiana,
Mr. Deshee, the preacher, teaches the creation story to his
class of young children, describing Heaven as he imagines it.

Scene II:

The scene changes to Heaven, where the Angels are
having a fish fry. The Angel Gabriel cries out, "Gangway
for de Lawd God Jehovah," and God himself joins the party.
He "rares back" and works a few miracles, then creates the
Earth and makes Adam in his image.

Scene III:

The Lawd visits Adam, creates Eve, and exhorts
them to leave the Tree alone.

Scene IV:

On his next visit to his creation, God discovers Cain
standing over the body of his brother Abel.

Scene V:

Cain, on God's advice, goes to town to settle down
and bring up a family. In the city, he meets a "sassy
wench," not at all the sort of girl de Lawd had in mind for
him.

Scene VI:

Back in his office, God admits to Gabriel that he has
stopped thinking about Mankind and regards the whole experi-
ment as a bad job. On an impulse, however, he decides to

visit Earth once again.

Scene VII:

To his intense displeasure, the Lawd finds the Earth a hotbed of sin and disobedience. The only decent man he sees is the preacher Noah.

Scene VIII:

God, while having supper with Noah and his family, discloses his plan to punish the wicked with a flood and instructs Noah and his sons to build the ark.

Scene IX:

Just as Noah finishes the ark--amid the jeers of his neighbors--the first drops begin to fall.

Scene X:

After the rain stops, the ark comes to rest and Noah and his family get out. God, pleased with the idea of a new start for men on Earth, tells Gabriel that he feels responsible for the future of mankind since the creation was his idea, but Gabriel has his doubts.

Part II

Scene I:

When the Lawd discovers that men have slipped back into their sinful ways, he decides not to destroy them again; rather, he will deliver the children of Abraham, Isaac, and Jacob from bondage in Egypt and give them Canaan, hoping that landowning will reform them.

Scene II:

God visits Moses and commissions him, together with Aaron, to make Pharaoh set the Hebrews free.

Scene III:

After Moses performs the tricks God has taught him, Pharaoh reluctantly agrees to let the Children of Israel follow Moses into the wilderness.

Scene IV:

As the Hebrews reach the Jordan, Moses, realizing
that he cannot enter the Promised Land, turns his people
over to Joshua. God appears to take Moses back to Heaven
with him.

Scene V:

The Children of Israel, now in captivity in Babylon
and as sinful as ever, are forsaken by God, who has grown
weary of waiting for them to improve.

Scene VI:

True to his word, God abandons the Israelites. During the Siege of Jerusalem, however, he listens to a few
prayers from below--especially those of a man called Hezdrel. Finally, overcome by a good man's plea, God decides
to visit the scene of the battle.

Scene VII:

Hezdrel, a soldier in the Hebrew army, does not
recognize God. He explains that the Hebrews have faith
because Hosea taught them that the old God of wrath and
vengeance--the God of Moses--has been replaced by a God
of mercy and love. When God asks Hezdrel how they came
to know this God of mercy, he replies, "Through suffering."

Scene VIII:

After His return to Heaven, God ponders Hezdrel's
words. He decides that He, too, must suffer if mankind is
to be redeemed. The play ends with God's vision of his son
Jesus bearing his cross to Calvary.

Theatre History and Popular Response:

The Green Pastures, like Street Scene, was a gamble
that paid off. Suggested by Roark Bradford's Ol' Man Adam
an' His Chillun, the play seemed to many a daring venture,
entirely too off-beat for commercial success. But when it
opened at the Mansfield Theatre on February 26, 1930, it
was greeted with rave notices and had a spectacular run of
540 performances on Broadway. Only one reviewer lodged

a lukewarm protest; the others called it a play of "surpassing beauty," "the divine comedy of the American theatre." One said simply, "I am too shaken by it to more than blurt out that The Green Pastures has done something which has never been done before." For representative reviews, see: Commonweal, March 19, 1930, p. 561; Nation, March 26, 1930, p. 376; New Republic, March 18, 1930, pp. 128-129; Theatre Arts, May, 1930, pp. 369-370.

Critical Reputation:

        Marcus Cook Connelly (1890-   ), born at McKeesport, Pennsylvania, began his career as a reporter for various Pittsburgh, Pennsylvania papers, but went to New York in 1915 to see a production of a musical comedy for which he had written the lyrics. The play failed, but Connelly, without funds for the trip back home, remained in New York. Shortly thereafter, he met George S. Kaufman and together they wrote several successful plays--Dulcy (1921), Merton of the Movies (1922), and Beggar on Horseback (1924). Connelly has had a long and active life as a man of letters but his fame will probably rest solidly upon The Green Pastures. Although Connelly's work is discussed in the standard studies of American drama, the only book length appraisal of his art and his place in American literature is Paul T. Nolan's Marc Connelly, 1969. For a collection of essays on The Green Pastures, see the 1963 edition of the play, which contains an introduction and conclusion by Vincent Long and critical essays by W. R. Matthews, John MacMurray, and Henry Self. The play has also been the subject of several critical articles, viz., Nick A. Ford's "How Genuine is The Green Pastures?," Phylon, XX (1959), 67-70; John T. Krumpelmann's "Marc Connelly's The Green Pastures and Goethe's Faust," Studies in Comparative Literature, W. F. McNair, ed., 199-218; Paul T. Nolan's "God on Stage: A Problem in Characterization in Marc Connelly's Green Pastures," Xavier University Studies, IV (1965), 75-84; Paul T. Nolan's "The Green Pastures: 'Behin' De Times'," Dramatics, XLII (March, 1971), 17, 20-21; Robert Withington's "Notes on the Corpus Christi Plays and The Green Pastures," Shakespeare Association Bulletin, IX (1934), 194-197.

The Theatre Season of

1930-1931

The Pulitzer Prize for this season went to Alison's
House, by Susan Glaspell, a play based on a romanticized
life of Emily Dickinson. The play, neither a critical nor a
commercial success, managed nevertheless to defeat Elizabeth the Queen, Once in a Lifetime, Tomorrow and Tomorrow, Green Grow the Lilacs and Five-Star Final.

ALISON'S HOUSE

Characters:

Ann Leslie   Eben
Jennie   Elsa
Richard Knowles   Miss Agatha
Ted Stanhope   Hodges
Louise   Mrs. Hodges
The Father

Act I:

On the last day of the 19th Century, the Stanhope
family prepares to leave its old home in Iowa. The house
is precious to them because Alison Stanhope, a poet, had
lived, written and, eighteen years before, died there. Alison,
a recluse, had posthumously achieved an international reputation. Neither Alison's brother John nor her sister Agatha,
now rather senile, wants outsiders to know that Alison had
been in love with a married man. When a reporter, Richard
Knowles, comes begging for a last look at Alison's room,
only Ann, Mr. Stanhope's secretary, and Ted, the youngest
son of the family, want to help him. Agatha, unnerved over
the presence of a stranger, tries to set fire to the room in
a futile attempt to destroy Alison's papers. At this point,
John's daughter Elsa, now in the bad graces of the family
because she has run away with a married man, returns to

make her good-byes to the old house. She receives a lukewarm welcome.

Act II:

        Just before Aunt Agatha collapses and dies of a heart
attack, she gives Elsa a portfolio of Alison's papers--the
very ones she had earlier attempted to burn.

Act III:

        In Alison's room, the Stanhopes discover that the
portfolio contains poems never before seen by the family,
poems that reveal the passion and anguish of Alison's
thwarted affair. Fearing a scandal, Stanhope wants to burn
the poems, but Elsa, to whom the poems have a special
significance, argues that they belong to the world. Stanhope, himself once hopelessly in love with Ann's mother,
finally agrees that the poems should be published.

Theatre History and Popular Response:

        Alison's House opened at the Civic Repertory Thea-
tre on December 1, 1930, and until it received the Pulitzer
Prize, was performed once or twice a week by Eva LeGal-
lienne's company. Thereafter, the play moved to the Ritz
but ran for only another two weeks, about 41 performances
in all. The critics did not receive it enthusiastically.
Many complained that although the story contained the germ
of a good play, Alison's House was dull, pompous, and
heavy-handed. The Pulitzer Prize Jury was roundly criticized for this selection. For representative reviews, see:
Commonweal, December 17, 1930, p. 187; Nation, May 27,
1931, pp. 590-591; Outlook, December 31, 1930, p. 711;
Theatre Arts, February, 1931, p. 99.

Critical Reputation:

        Susan Glaspell (1882-1948), a native of Davenport,
Iowa, studied at Drake University, then worked as a newspaper reporter, but soon quit to devote herself to writing.
In 1913 she married George Cram Cook, a playwright, and
together they worked in the Little Theatre Movement and
organized the Provincetown Players. During her lifetime,
Miss Glaspell was an actress, a producer, a writer of short

stories, novels, and non-fiction, but she is perhaps best re-
membered for her work in the Little Theatre Movement.
For a biographical sketch see Kunitz and Haycraft's Twentieth
Century Authors, 1942.   For an early appraisal of her work,
see Thomas Dickinson's Playwrights of the New American
Theatre, 1924, pp. 208-218.   Arthur E. Waterman's Susan
Glaspell, 1966, is a recent critical biography.   Alison's
House has received little scholarly attention.

The Theatre Season of

1931-1932

The Pulitzer Prize went this season, for the first time in its history, to a musical comedy--Of Thee I Sing by George S. Kaufman and Morrie Ryskind. This breezy satire on American politics and political attitudes beat out some formidable competition: Mourning Becomes Electra, The House of Connelly, Reunion in Vienna, Counsellor-at-Law, and The Animal Kingdom.

OF THEE I SING

Characters:

Louis Lippman	Vladimir Vidovitch
Francis X. Gilhooley	Yussef Yussevitch
Maid	The Chief Justice
Matthew Arnold Fulton	Scrubwoman
Sen. Robert E. Lyons	The French Ambassador
Sen. Carver Jones	Senate Clerk
Alexander Throttlebottom	Guide
John P. Wintergreen	Photographers, Policemen,
Sam Jenkins	Supreme Court Justices,
Diana Devereaux	Secretaries, Sight-seers,
Mary Turner	Newspapermen, Senators,
Miss Benson	Flunkeys, Guests, etc.

Act I

Scene I:

The progress of a political parade across the stage proclaims Wintergreen the party's candidate for President.

Scene II:

In the smoke-filled rooms, Wintergreen and his party search for a popular issue. Remembering that all the world

loves a lover, they decide that Wintergreen will fall in love
with and marry the winner of a national beauty contest.

Scene III:

Miss Diana Devereaux, a Southern belle, wins the
contest, but in the meantime, Wintergreen has fallen in love
with a pretty little secretary, Mary Turner, whose great
talent is her ability to make corn muffins. The only one
not pleased with this turn of events is Miss Devereaux, who
threatens to sue.

Scene IV:

John and Mary campaign vigorously; in fact, John
proposes and Mary accepts in each of the 48 states.

Scene V:

John is swept into office by a commanding majority,
the public being unable to resist a campaign based on love.

Scene VI:

John is inaugurated and married on the same day.
Diana appears to plead her case, but the Supreme Court declares corn muffins the winner and advises Diana to forget
her grievances.

Act II

Scene I:

John and Mary take over the leadership of the country amid rumors that sympathy for Miss Devereaux's cause
is spreading. Even the French Ambassador appears to say
his government supports her claim; she is, it seems, the
"illegitimate daughter of an illegitimate son of an illegitimate
nephew of Napoleon."

Scene II:

John seems on the verge of impeachment, and his
followers wonder who will take his place. No one can remember the Vice-President, one Alexander Throttlebottom.

Scene III:

     Mary proclaims that she is going to have a baby,
and since no precedent for impeaching an expectant father
exists, her announcement saves the day.

Scene IV:

     The French demand that the Wintergreens agree to
give the baby to France to bolster its sagging growth rate,
but this Wintergreen refuses to consider.

Scene V:

     With "posterity just around the corner," the great
and near-great assemble to await news of the First Lady's
confinement. Mary produces twins, Diana reappears and
wins Throttlebottom as a consolation prize, and John Wintergreen, the candidate extolling love, is the Man of the Hour.

Theatre History and Popular Response:

     An immediate success which ran for 441 performances,
Of Thee I Sing opened at the Music Box Theatre in December of 1931. The play was wildly acclaimed by most reviewers, not only for the brilliance of its score (by George
and Ira Gershwin) and embellishments, but for the keenness
of its satire as well. Some critics grumbled, however,
when Of Thee I Sing won the Pulitzer instead of O'Neill's
trilogy Mourning Becomes Electra. For representative reviews, see: Catholic World, February, 1932, pp. 587-588;
Literary Digest, January 16, 1932, p. 18; Nation, January
13, 1932, p. 56; New Republic, January 13, 1932, p. 243.

Critical Reputation:

     George S. Kaufman (1889-1961), born in Pittsburgh,
Pennsylvania, and educated in public schools, came to the
theatre after trying law school and the business world.
Disappointed in both, he became a newspaper reporter and
then drama editor of the New York Times, a position he
held long after he began his career as playwright. He
wrote one play without a collaborator--The Butter and Egg
Man (1925); the rest of his successful work was done in collaboration with such people as Marc Connelly, Moss Hart,

Edna Ferber, Ring Lardner, Alexander Woollcott, Abe Burrows and others.

Morrie Ryskind (1895-   ), a native New Yorker who
attended public schools and who graduated from Columbia,
was, like Kaufman, a newspaperman as well as a playwright.
In addition to Of Thee I Sing, he and Kaufman wrote Animal
Crackers (1929), Strike Up the Band (1930), and a sequel to
Of Thee I Sing entitled Let Them Eat Cake (1933).

Ryskind was overshadowed by his famous partner, and
he received little serious critical attention. Kaufman, one
of the American theatre's most successful and influential
figures, receives attention in the major studies of American
drama and in some of the critical journals as well. See,
for example, Burns Mantle's "George S. Kaufman," in American Playwrights of Today, 1938; Joseph Mersand's chapter
"George S. Kaufman: Master of Technique," in The American
Drama Since 1930, 1951; and George Jean Nathan's "George
S. Kaufman," in The Theatre in the Fifties, 1953. Two
articles in scholarly journals are R. W. Lembke's "The
George S. Kaufman Plays as Social History," Quarterly
Journal of Speech, XXXIII (Oct., 1947), 341-347 and Montrose J. Moses's "George S. Kaufman," North American Re-
view, CCXXXVII (1934), 76-83.

For discussions on Of Thee I Sing, consult John Mason Brown's Two on the Aisle, 1938, 282-286; and John Cor-
bin's "George Kaufman," Saturday Review, IX (January 21,
1933), 385-386. Biographical sketches of both Kaufman and
Ryskind can be found in The Biographical Encyclopedia and
Who's Who of the American Theatre, 1966.

The Theatre Season of

1932-1933

Maxwell Anderson's reformist play Both Your Houses, a scathing attack on corruption in government, received the Pulitzer Prize for this season. It was the only Pulitzer Prize Anderson was ever to win, but many Broadway observers thought Both Your Houses his worst play. The also-rans were: One Sunday Afternoon, Dinner at Eight, We, the People, Alien Corn and Biography.

BOTH YOUR HOUSES

Characters:

Marjorie Gray	Dell
Bus	Sneden
Eddie Wister	Miss McMurtry
Solomon Fitzmaurice	Wingblatt
Mark	Peebles
Simeon Gray	Farnum
Levering	Alan McClean
Merton	Ebner

Act I:

When idealistic young Alan McClean, a schoolteacher from Nevada, comes to Congress for the first time, he is appalled at the rampant greed and dishonesty he finds in Washington. As a member of the Appropriations Committee, he discovers that his colleagues have tacked on various "pork barrel" projects to a bill which originally stood at $40,000,000, bringing the figure up to a staggering $275,000,000. When the Committee, fearing a Presidential veto of so large a sum, tries to cut the figure down, McClean offers to give up a much needed irrigation project for his home state. Several members of the committee, amused at his naivete, tell him in so many words that bribery is the modus oper-

46

andi in Congress. McClean, fighting mad, enlists the aid
of Bus, a secretary who knows the ropes, and vows to defeat
the bill.

Act II:

Alan decides to overload the bill and run the figure
so high that no one would dare sponsor or vote for it.
Simeon Gray, the chairman of the committee, desperately
needs the passage of the bill, which contains money for a
penitentiary in his district, a project designed to save a
shaky bank and keep Gray himself out of jail.

Act III:

Gray's daughter Marjorie appeals to Alan to sacrifice
his crusade in order to save her father, but Alan refuses.
In spite of his efforts, however, the monstrous bill passes
the house by more than the two-thirds majority necessary to
override the President's veto. McClean, shaken by the
depth of the corruption in government, predicts that someday the voters will become disgusted enough to rise up and
throw the rascals out.

Theatre History and Popular Response:

Both Your Houses opened at the Royale Theatre on
March 6, 1933, and ran for 120 performances, in spite of
the fact that the theme--corruption in government--seemed
irrelevant to many playgoers during the first wave of enthu-
siasm that greeted Franklin Roosevelt's inauguration, an
event which took place only three days before Anderson's
play opened. The notices were mixed. While no critic
considered it a great play, some said it was "competent
enough"; others simply dismissed it as a bore, a play lacking impetus, dramatic tension, or poetic thrust. For representative reviews, see: Literary Digest, March 25, 1933,
p. 15; Nation, March 29, 1933, p. 355; New Republic,
March 29, 1933, p. 188; Theatre Arts, May, 1933, pp. 338-
340.

Critical Reputation:

Maxwell Anderson (1888-1959) was born in Atlantic,
Pennsylvania, the son of a clergyman. He received the

B.A. from the University of North Dakota in 1911 and the
M.A. from Stanford in 1914. Like so many playwrights, he
began his career as a newspaperman. His first great success in the theatre was What Price Glory? (1924), written
in collaboration with Laurence Stallings, also a newspaperman turned playwright. Anderson's later attempt to create
a modern verse drama makes him a controversial figure in
the history of the American literature. Some critics consider him one of America's most distinguished playwrights,
second only to Eugene O'Neill; others think his work utterly
lacking in distinction. Nevertheless, his plays have created
considerable critical interest. Two bibliographical studies
are available: Martha Cox's Maxwell Anderson Bibliography,
1958, and Vedder Gilbert's "The Career of Maxwell Anderson: A Checklist of Books and Articles," Modern Drama, II
(1960), 386-394. An early study of his work which is still
useful is Barrett H. Clark's Maxwell Anderson: The Man
and His Plays, 1933. For a recent study, see Mabel D.
Bailey's Maxwell Anderson: The Playwright as Prophet,
1957. He figures prominently in many major studies of
American drama, and dozens of articles in scholarly journals discuss his philosophy, his poetics, his position in the
theatre. Both Your Houses is not considered one of his important plays, but is discussed in John Mason Brown's Two
on the Aisle, 1938, and Gerald Rabkin's Drama and Commitment, 1964, pp. 270-272.

The Theatre Season of

1933-1934

When the Pulitzer Prize went this season to Sidney Kingsley's medical melodrama, Men in White, the three Pulitzer jurors resigned in disgust. Although they had unanimously recommended Maxwell Anderson's Mary of Scotland, the Advisory Board, a group of newspaper editors with little knowledge of the drama, according to their outraged critics, overturned the decision. In addition to Mary of Scotland the other contenders were: Ah, Wilderness!, Dodsworth, Yellow Jack, Wednesday's Child, They Shall Not Die and Tobacco Road.

MEN IN WHITE

Characters:

Dr. Gordon	Dr. Otis (Shorty)
Dr. Hochberg	Dr. Bradley (Pete)
Dr. Michaelson	Dr. Crawford (Mac)
Dr. Vitale	Barbara Dennin
Dr. McCabe	Nurse Jamison
Dr. Ferguson	Nurse Mary Ryan
Dr. Wren	First Nurse
Second Nurse	Dorothy Smith
Orderly	Mrs. Smith
Mr. Hudson	Mr. Smith
James Mooney	Mr. Houghton
Laura Hudson	Mr. Spencer
Dr. Levine	Mr. Rummond
Dr. Cunningham	Mrs. D'Andrea

Act I:

Dr. George Ferguson, a student of the scholarly and dedicated surgeon, Dr. Hochberg, works so hard at the hospital that he has little time for his rich, spoiled fiancee, Laura Hudson. They finally quarrel when she demands that

49

he give up his fierce ambition to be a great surgeon and settle down to ordinary doctoring. On the night of the quarrel,
a lonely student nurse, Barbara Dennin, comes to Ferguson's
room, ostensibly to borrow some notes, and Ferguson makes
love to her.

Act II:

Three months later, Barbara, pregnant from her one
encounter with Ferguson, has a badly botched abortion which
necessitates a hysterectomy. Ferguson learns of her problem for the first time when he has to perform the operation.
Laura, a spectator in the operating room, discovers the relationship between Ferguson and the girl.

Act III:

Ferguson vows he will marry Barbara even though it
means sacrificing his career. Barbara dies, however, leaving him free to pursue his studies in Vienna. Laura wants
him to reconsider his decision, but when she sees his determination, she gives up and Ferguson goes relentlessly
back to work.

Theatre History and Reviews:

Men in White had a run of 351 performances after its
opening at the Broadhurst Theatre on September 26, 1933.
On the whole, the play did not receive bad notices at first,
but angry cries arose after the play won the Pulitzer Prize.
Some first-night critics called it an "engrossing play," a
"serious and gripping new drama." Others were less en-
thusiastic; John Mason Brown, for example, said the only
detail overlooked was an anaesthetic for the audience. For
representative reviews, see: Commonweal, October 13,
1933, pp. 563-564; Nation, October 11, 1933, pp. 419-420;
New Republic, October 11, 1933, pp. 241-242; Theatre Arts,
December, 1933, pp. 915-916.

Critical Reputation:

Kingsley, born Sidney Kieschner (1906-), a native
of New York, attended Cornell University where he became
interested in the drama. Associated with the theatre all of
his adult life as writer, director and producer, he is best

known for his plays Dead End (1935), Detective Story (1949),
The Patriots (see entry for 1942-1943) and his adaptation of
Arthur Koestler's novel, Darkness at Noon (see entry for
1950-1951). Two of his more recent plays are Lunatics and
Lovers (1954) and Night Life (1962). Kingsley has had phe-
nomenal commercial successes, but his plays have attracted
little scholarly interest. See Kunitz and Haycraft's Twentieth
Century Authors, 1942, for an account of his life. Allen
Lewis discusses his work in American Plays and Playwrights,
1965, pp. 148-151; otherwise, he receives only passing references in the major studies of American drama. For an
essay on Men in White, the prototype of the "soap opera-
medic" show, see John Mason Brown's Two on the Aisle,
1938, pp. 171-173.

The Theatre Season of

1934-1935

In 1934-35 the Pulitzer Prize committee made another unpopular award, this time to Zoe Akins's The Old Maid, adapted from Edith Wharton's short story of the same name. Nearly everyone agreed that Lillian Hellman's play The Children's Hour should have won, but apparently, the Pulitzer jurors were reluctant to reward a play with a taboo theme-- Lesbianism. Also passed over were: Awake and Sing, The Petrified Forest, Valley Forge, Rain from Heaven, The Farmer Takes a Wife, and Merrily We Roll Along.

THE OLD MAID

Characters:

Delia Lovell	Joseph Ralston
Charlotte Lovell	James Ralston
Mrs. Jennie Meade	Servant
Bridget	Dee
Clementina	John Halsey
Dr. Lanskell	Lanning Halsey
Mrs. Mingott	Tina

First Episode:

In 1833, Delia Lovell marries James Ralston, a man with money and social position, instead of Clem Spender, an artist with an uncertain future. Her cousin Charlotte, in love with Clem herself, cannot understand Delia's choice.

Second Episode:

Six years later, Charlotte has established a day nursery for indigent children, one of whom is the "hundred dollar baby," a white child left on the doorstep of a Negro couple with a hundred dollar bill pinned to its dress. Char-

lotte is planning to marry Delia's brother-in-law, Joseph,
but he insists that she give up her nursery.

Third Episode:

Charlotte tells Delia that she cannot give up the nursery because the "hundred dollar baby" is her own child,
conceived on Delia's wedding day during a brief affair with
Clem Spender, Delia's old suitor. She bore the child during
a trip down South, which she ostensibly made to cure a lung
complaint. Delia, convinced that Charlotte and Joe should
not marry, tells Joe that her cousin's lung trouble has re-
curred. She also arranges for a house where Charlotte and
the child, can live together.

Fourth Episode:

Fourteen years later, after her husband's death,
Delia has moved Tina and Charlotte under her roof and has
managed to steal Tina's affection away from Charlotte, an
easy feat since Charlotte is now a grim, unattractive old
maid, soured by the secret she carries. Finally, Charlotte
reluctantly agrees to let Delia adopt Tina, giving her the
name and money to make a socially acceptable marriage.

Fifth Episode:

On the night before Tina's wedding, Charlotte considers telling Tina the truth, but does not. Delia will not
tell either, but admonishes Tina to be kinder to her "Aunt"
Charlotte.

History and Reviews:

The Old Maid opened at the Empire Theatre on January 7, 1935, and ran for 305 performances. The critics received it rather unenthusiastically, complaining of its diffuse-
ness, its wordiness, its thinness. As one critic put it, the
play had been adapted "to the vanishing point...." For representative reviews, see: Catholic World, February, 1935,
p. 602; Commonweal, January 25, 1935, p. 375; New Republic, March 20, 1935, p. 82; Theatre Arts, March, 1935, p.
176.

Critical Reputation:

     Zoe Akins (1896-1958), born in Humansville, Mis-
souri, and educated in private schools, was always interested
in the theatre. An actress turned playwright, she wrote
Papa (1916), Declassee (1919), Daddy's Gone A-Hunting
(1921) and The Texas Nightingale (1922). Winning the Pulitzer Prize did not, however, prevent her decline and final
descent into obscurity. Twentieth Century Authors, 1942,
by Kunitz and Haycraft, contains the best account of her
life; passing references to her plays appear in the standard
histories of American drama. See especially Dickinson's
Playwrights of the New American Theatre, 1924, pp. 208-
218, and Quinn's A History of The American Drama, 1927,
pp. 141-144, for a brief discussion of some of her plays.
See also "Window Shopping Through Life with Zoe Akins,"
by John Mason Brown in his Two on the Aisle, 1938, pp.
145-147. There has been little scholarly interest in The
Old Maid.

The Theatre Season of

1935-1936

The Pulitzer Prize went this season to Robert E.
Sherwood's play Idiot's Delight, a decision which Broadway
observers considered reasonable. By this time, however,
the New York drama critics, disgusted with the previous
Pulitzer Prizes given to such plays as Alison's House, Men
in White and The Old Maid, had banded together to give
their own annual award--The New York Drama Critics Circle
Award--as a corrective. The first recipient of the new
award was Maxwell Anderson's verse tragedy, Winterset.
Also contending that year were First Lady, Paradise Lost,
Dead End, End of Summer, Porgy and Bess and Ethan
Frome.

IDIOT'S DELIGHT

Characters:

Dumptsy	Dr. Waldersee
Orchestra Leader	Mr. Cherry
Donald Vavadel	Mrs. Cherry
Pittaluga	Harry Van
Auguste	Shirley
Captain Locicero	Beulah
Bebe	Fourth Officer
Francine	Quillery
Elaine	Signor Rossi
Edna	Signora Rossi
Major	Maid
First Officer	Achille Weber
Second Officer	Irene
Third Officer	

Act I:

At the outbreak of World War II, a strange collection
of international travelers are trapped together in a third-rate

resort hotel near the border--soon to be closed--of Switzer-
land and Austria. Harry Van, an American Song and Dance
man touring Europe with six dancing girls, Les Blondes,
meets Irene, the mistress of Achille Weber, a French muni-
tions maker. Although Irene passes herself off as a White
Russian countess, Harry believes she is his lost love, a
vaudeville performer with whom he spent one memorable
night in a hotel in Omaha. Completing the party are a pair
of British newlyweds, a radical Frenchman, and a German
doctor frantically trying to cross the border to finish an ex-
periment on some cancerous rats.

Act II:

Harry and Les Blondes do their act in the evening,
hoping to distract the edgy guests from the rumors of war.
Quillery, the radical Frenchman, bursts in and cries that
Paris has been bombed, and denounces the group for singing
and dancing while the City of Light burns. When Quillery
also denounces the Fascists, the Italian soldiers drag him
away and shoot him. Later, Harry tells Irene that he remembers her from Omaha, but Irene, vastly amused, rather
unconvincingly denies the story.

Act III:

Because of the Italian bombardment of Paris, re-
prisal raids on the airfield near the hotel are shortly expected. Everyone who can get out tries to leave. Weber
abandons Irene, who has accused him of being a merchant
of death. The others escape, but Harry, after seeing his
girls to safety, rejoins Irene. As the bombs begin to fall,
Harry and Irene, old lovers reunited, drink champagne while
Harry bangs out "Onward Christian Soldiers" on the piano.

Theatre History and Popular Response:

Idiot's Delight opened at the Schubert Theatre on
March 24, 1936, and ran for 300 performances. The critical consensus was that the play was a well crafted piece
about a serious subject and a superb bit of entertainment
with equal parts of moral allegory and fizzy comedy which
somehow miraculously added up to a good play. For representative reviews, see: Nation, April 15, 1936, pp. 490-
492; Saturday Review, May 9, 1936, pp. 6-7; Theatre Arts,
May, 1936, pp. 340-341; Time, April 6, 1936, p. 38.

Critical Reputation:

Robert E. Sherwood (1896-1955), three-time winner
of the Pulitzer Prize for Drama, was born in New Rochelle,
New York, the child of a wealthy investment broker and a
painter. Educated at Milton Academy and Harvard, he became a writer for various New York magazines and news-
papers until he began to devote most of his time to playwriting. Passionately interested in politics, he was a
speechwriter for Franklin Roosevelt and an assistant to the
Secretary of the Navy and to the Secretary of War during
Roosevelt's administration. He received the Pulitzer Prize
for History for his book Roosevelt and Hopkins (1948).

Three book-length studies deal with Sherwood's life
and art. An authoritative biography is John Mason Brown's
The Worlds of Robert E. Sherwood: Mirror to His Times,
1896-1939, 1965. The first full-length critical study is R.
Baird Shuman's Robert E. Sherwood, 1964; the most recent
one is W. J. Meserve's Robert E. Sherwood: Reluctant
Moralist, 1970. Both of the critical books contain bibliographies and both discuss Idiot's Delight at length.

WINTERSET

Characters:

Trock Estrella	Judge Gaunt
Shadow	Carr
Lucio	Mio
Piny	Sailor
Miriamne	Radical
Garth	Policeman
Esdras	Sergeant
First Girl	Two Young Men in Serge
Second Girl	Two Street Urchins
Hobo	

Act I:

When Mio Romagna, son of a confessed anarchist
recently executed for murder, comes to a dingy tenement
looking for Garth Esdras, a witness he thinks can clear his
father's name, he meets Miriamne, Garth's sister. They
fall in love at once, but when Miriamne realizes who Mio is,
she begs him to go away. She knows her brother saw the

gangster Trock Estrella commit the murder Romagna died
for, but to avoid implicating himself, Garth remained silent
during the trial.

Act II:

        That same evening Judge Gaunt, who presided at the
Romagna trial, comes into the neighborhood.   Now half
crazed because he sent an innocent man to his death, the
old judge talks incessantly about the case.   Garth and his
father, Rabbi Esdras, take Gaunt inside to protect him from
Estrella, who watches Garth closely.   When Mio arrives,
looking for Garth, he discovers Miriamne is Garth's sister.
Mio then conducts a mock trial, wringing from Estrella the
admission that he, not Romagna, committed the murder.
When the police arrive, Miriamne, who must decide between
protecting Garth or substantiating Mio's story, tells a lie to
save her brother.

Act III:

        Miriamne follows Mio into the street where they de-
clare their love for each other.   Mio has lost his thirst for
revenge and decides not to tell what he knows since the
truth would hurt Miriamne's family.   Trock Estrella's men
gun Mio down anyway, and when Miriamne cries out that
she will tell the story to the world, they shoot her as well.
Rabbi Esdras tells Garth over the body of his daughter that
it is better to die young, for love, than to grow old in a
meaningless world.

Theatre History and Popular Response:

        Winterset opened at the Martin Beck Theatre in New
York on September 25, 1935, and ran for 179 performances.
While the play was not an overwhelming success, reviewers
were awed by Anderson's attempt to make poetic drama out
of modern material.   He failed, one said, because he attempted the impossible.   Others agreed that although the
play was pretentious, contrived, and dull in spots, it nevertheless enriched the season.   For representative reviews,
see: Literary Digest, October 5, 1935, p. 20; Nation, October 9, 1935, p. 420; New Republic, October 16, p. 274;
Theatre Arts, November, 1935, pp. 815-820.

<u>Critical Reputation</u>:

For general information on Anderson's life and his place in the history of American drama, see the entry for 1932-1933. Bailey's <u>Maxwell Anderson</u> contains a discussion of <u>Winterset</u>, pp. 132-142, and numerous critical articles on the play have appeared in scholarly publications: Francis E. Abernathy's "Winterset: A Modern Revenge Tragedy," <u>Modern Drama</u>, VII (1964), 185-189; Jacob H. Adler's "Shakespeare in <u>Winterset</u>," Educational Theatre Journal, VI (1954), 241-248; Benjamin Boyce's "Anderson's <u>Winterset</u>," Explicator, II (February, 1944) Item 32; William Davenport's "Anderson's <u>Winterset</u>," Explicator, X (1952), Item 41; Ainslie Harris's "Maxwell Anderson," Madison Quarterly, IV (1944), 30-44; Samuel Klinger's "Hebraic Lore in Maxwell Anderson's <u>Winterset</u>," American Literature, XVIII (1946), 219-232; J. T. McCullen's "Two Quests for Truth: King Oedipus and <u>Winterset</u>," Laurel Review, V (1965), 28-35; Howard Pearce's "Job in Anderson's <u>Winterset</u>," Modern Drama, VI (1963), 32-41; and Robert Roby's "Two Worlds: Maxwell Anderson's <u>Winterset</u>," College English, XVIII (1957), 195-202.

The Theatre Season of

1936-1937

The Pulitzer Prize went this season to the widely acclaimed comedy, You Can't Take It With You, by George Kaufman and Moss Hart. Although the reviewers had received it with salvos of praise, many of them later criticized the Pulitzer Committee for choosing the zany box office success over more serious plays. The second Circle award given by the New York Drama Critics went again to Maxwell Anderson, this time for his play High Tor. Also running were Johnny Johnson, Excursion, The Women and Having Wonderful Time.

YOU CAN'T TAKE IT WITH YOU

Characters:

Penelope Sycamore	Henderson
Essie	Tony Kirby
Rheba	Boris Kolenkhov
Paul Sycamore	Gay Wellington
Mr. De Pinna	Mr. Kirby
Ed	Mrs. Kirby
Donald	Three Men
Martin Vanderhof	Olga
Alice	

Act I:

Right around the corner from Columbia University lives Martin Vanderhof and his bizarre but engaging family. Martin collects snakes, goes to commencement exercises, and refuses on principle to pay his income taxes. His daughter, Penny Sycamore, paints and writes plays; her husband, Paul, makes fireworks in the cellar; her daughter, Essie, studies ballet with a crusty old White Russian; Essie's husband, Ed, prints and plays the xylophone. Penny's other daughter, Alice, actually has a job and is dating the boss's son, Tony Kirby. Alice tries to keep her relationship with Tony from becoming serious because she fears that her mad family--which she adores--will make a bad impression on Tony's parents.

Act II:

A week later, Alice's suspicions are confirmed when the Kirbys come for dinner on the wrong night and find the Vanderhof crew insanely busy with its various pursuits. The stuffy Kirbys are appalled by the irregularity of the household, especially when agents from the justice department, investigating some revolutionary literature that Ed has printed for practice, discover the gunpowder in the cellar and throw the whole group in jail.

Act III:

The next day, Alice, in despair, plans to move out. She refuses to see Tony, who insists he still wants to marry her. The ballet teacher brings in the Grand Duchess Olga, now a waitress at Childs Restaurant, who insists on cooking the dinner. Meanwhile, Mr. Kirby arrives, determined to make Tony come home with him. When Grandpa explains his philosophy of life to Mr. Kirby and chides him for selling stocks and bonds when he could be getting fun out of life, Kirby, finally reconciled to Tony and Alice's marriage, stays for a dinner of the Grand Duchess's blintzes.

Theatre History and Popular Response:

You Can't Take It With You opened at the Booth Theatre on December 14, 1936, and had a long run of 837 performances. The notices were filled with adulation; cross words were only heard when the same critics who had previously praised the play decided it was too lightweight to receive the Pulitzer Prize. For representative reviews, see: Commonweal, December 25, 1936, p. 249; New Republic, December 30, 1936, p. 273; Newsweek, December 26, 1936, p. 38; Theatre Arts, February, 1937, pp. 96-97.

Critical Reputation:

For a general introduction to the life and work of

George Kaufman, see the 1931-1932 entry. Moss Hart (1904-
1961), Kaufman's most important collaborator, was a native
of New York City and was educated in its public schools.
His early interest in the theatre led him into acting, writing
and directing. As a result of the three distinguished comedies written with Kaufman--Once in a Lifetime (1930), You
Can't Take It With You, and The Man Who Came to Dinner
(1939), he and Kaufman established themselves as the most
incisive satirists in the American theatre. Hart has not,
however, received as much critical attention as Kaufman.
For a sketch of his life and work, consult Kunitz and Haycraft's Twentieth Century Authors, 1942; see also the major
studies of American drama, especially Burns Mantle's Contemporary American Playwrights, 1938, and George Jean
Nathan's The Theatre in the Fifties, 1953. An article which
discusses his career is Rosamund Gilder's "The Fabulous
Hart," in Theatre Arts, February, 1944, pp. 89-98.

        For a scholarly article on You Can't Take It With
You, see Charles Kaplan's "Two Depression Plays and
Broadway's Popular Idealism," Arizona Quarterly, XV (1963),
579-585.

                        HIGH TOR

Characters:

        The Indian   De Witt
        Van Van Dorn   Dope
        Judith   Elkus
        Art J. Biggs   Buddy
        Judge Skimmerhorn   Patsy
        Lise   A. B. Skimmerhorn
        Captain Asher   Budge
        Pieter   Dutch Crew of the Onrust
        A Sailor

Act I:

        Two crooked realtors, Biggs and Skimmerhorn, want
to buy and raze High Tor, a mountain overlooking the Hudson, but Van Van Dorn, a Thoreauvian figure who lives on
the property, refuses to sell. His sweetheart, Judith, disgusted with what she considers Van's aimlessness and lack
of business sense, declares that they are finished and leaves
him. Meanwhile, three bank robbers in hiding from the au-

thorities run into Biggs and Skimmerhorn, who accidently
end up with the satchel of money. Also present on the
mountain is the phantom crew of a Dutch ship lost during
Henry Hudson's expedition. The sailors agree to help Biggs
and Skimmerhorn get down the mountain, but instead trap
them high over a gorge in the basket of one of their own
steam shovels.

Act II:

    When Judith comes back looking for Van, she learns
that he has fallen in love with Lise, the wife of the Dutch
captain. Lise, realizing that their love can never be, goes
back with the crew when their ship returns, and Van and
Judith are reunited.

Act III:

    The police apprehend the two crooks with the money,
but before they are led away, they offer Van $50,000 for
the mountain. Van agrees to sell after an old Indian explains the futility of trying to block progress. Man's works
are transitory, he says, and nature soon covers up all evi-
dence of his presence.

Theatre History and Popular Response:

    High Tor, which opened at the Martin Beck Theatre
on January 9, 1937, and closed after 171 performances, was
warmly reviewed by the critics. They called it "a power-
fully imaginative comedy," a play to "flick the mind and
touch the heart." For representative reviews, see: Forum,
June, 1937, p. 353; Nation, June 30, 1937, p. 136; New
Republic, February 3, 1937, pp. 411-412; Time, January 18,
1937, p. 47.

Critical Reputation:

    A general introduction to Maxwell Anderson's life and
career appears under the entry for 1932-1933. For a discussion of High Tor, see pages 146-149 of Mabel Bailey's
Maxwell Anderson, 1957; and Gerald Rabkin's Drama and
Commitment, 1964, pp. 284-287.

The Theatre Season of

1937-1938

The Pulitzer Prize for this season went to Thornton
Wilder's play Our Town, which some now consider one of
the four or five best plays in American dramatic literature.
Its only serious contender was Steinbeck's Of Mice and Men,
which received the Critic's Circle Award. Other plays of
the season were Golden Boy, Susan and God, On Borrowed
Time, and Prologue to Glory.

OUR TOWN

Characters:

Stage Manager	Emily Webb
Dr. Gibbs	Professor Willard
Joe Crowell	Mr. Webb
Howie Newsome	Woman in the Balcony
Mrs. Gibbs	Man in the Auditorium
Mrs. Webb	Lady in the Box
George Gibbs	Simon Stimson
Rebecca Gibbs	Mrs. Soames
Wally Webb	Constable Warren
Si Crowell	Joe Stoddard
Baseball Players	People of the Town
Sam Craig	

Act I:

Our Town, which defies conventional summary, is
cemented together by the presence of the Stage Manager,
who remains onstage during the entire play, introducing the
characters, directing and interpreting the action, and playing
some of the parts himself. Set in Grover's Corners, New
Hampshire, Act One covers one day, May 7, 1901. Although
many characters are introduced and sketched--the milkman,
the paper boy, the choir director--the action focuses on two

families, those of Dr. Gibbs and Editor Webb. The editor's daughter, Emily, and the Doctor's son, George, appear to be falling in love.

Act II:

Act II, set in the year 1904, recreates the wedding day of George and Emily and also contains a flashback depicting the moment when George and Emily first became aware of their love.

Act III:

Nine years later, the Stage Manager shows the audience the cemetery where the dead sit quietly on a row of chairs. Emily, who has died in childbirth, takes her place beside Mrs. Gibbs. She finds the dead strangely resigned, but she longs to return to life. When the stage manager offers her a chance to relive one day in her life, she accepts, even though her companions advise against it, and chooses to return to the day of her twelfth birthday. During her journey back to childhood, she learns how little a person grasps of life, how little one understands of its transitory beauty. The experience is so painful to Emily that she begs the Stage Manager to let her return to the graveyard, and when George comes to fling himself on her grave, she sadly remarks on how little the living know.

Theatre History and Popular Response:

Wilder's unorthodox play opened at Henry Miller's Theatre on February 4, 1938, and ran for 336 performances. Oddly enough, the play, now an enduring and much beloved staple in the literature of American drama, did not receive the unanimous acclaim of critics. Although many considered it a deeply moving and poetic play, "lovely past all enduring" in the words of one, others complained that Wilder's attempt to attain cosmic significance was pretentious and strained. For representative reviews, see: Christian Century, August 3, 1938, pp. 943-944; Nation, February 19, 1938, pp. 224-225; New Republic, February 23, 1938, p. 74; Theatre Arts, March, 1938, pp. 172-173.

Critical Reputation:

      Thornton Wilder (1897-), born in Madison, Wisconsin, spent part of his boyhood in China where his father was consul general at Hong Kong and Shanghai. He did his undergraduate work at Berkeley, Oberlin, and Yale and received the M.A. from Princeton in 1925. A teacher as well as a writer, he has spent much of his professional life lecturing at the University of Chicago, Harvard, and various continental universities. Although his place in the history of American drama would be secure had he written nothing but Our Town, he also received two other Pulitzer Prizes--one in drama for The Skin of Our Teeth (see the entry at 1941-42) and one for his novel The Bridge of San Luis Rey (1927). His work is now a standard part of serious American literary scholarship. Three bibliographical guides are available: Jackson Bryer's "Thornton Wilder and the Reviewers," Papers of the Bibliographical Society of America, LVIII (1964), 34-49; Heinz Kosok's "Thornton Wilder: A Bibliography of Criticism," Twentieth Century Literature, IX (1963), 93-100; and J. M. Edelstein's A Bibliographical Checklist of the Writings of Thornton Wilder, 1959. Several recent full length critical treatments explore his life and art: Rex Burbank's Thornton Wilder, 1961; Malcolm Goldstein's The Art of Thornton Wilder, 1965; Bernard Grebanier's Thornton Wilder, 1964; and Donald Haberman's The Plays of Thornton Wilder, 1967. Two short pieces basic to an understanding of Wilder's work are Malcolm Cowley's "The Man Who Abolished Time," Saturday Review of Literature, October 6, 1956, pp. 13-14, 50-52; and Joseph Firebaugh's "The Humanism of Thornton Wilder," Pacific Spectator, IV (Autumn, 1950), 426-438.

      For scholarly articles which discuss Our Town see Arthur H. Ballet's "In Our Living and In Our Dying," English Journal, XLV (1956), 243-249; Winfield Scott's "Our Town and the Golden Veil," Virginia Quarterly Review, XXIX (January, 1953), 103-117, and George D. Stephen's "Our Town--Great American Tragedy?", Modern Drama, I (1959), 258-264. In addition, the book-length critical treatments of Wilder's work (cited above) contain discussions of the play.

OF MICE AND MEN

Characters:

George	Curley's Wife
Lennie	Slim
Candy	Carlson
The Boss	Whit
Curley	Crooks

Act I:

In the rich Salinas Valley of California, two migrant workers, George and his pathetic, feeble-minded companion, Lennie, move to a new job. At the last place, Lennie, a giant of a man who likes to fondle mice and puppies but always seems to crush them, got into trouble when he innocently tried to touch a girl's silk dress.

George and Lennie, hoping to save enough to buy a place of their own, are eager to work, but George senses that trouble may erupt with the new boss's quarrelsome son Curley, recently married to a flirtatious woman.

Act II:

George and Lennie's dream seems close to realization when Candy, an old crippled hand, offers to join them and agrees to contribute his savings. Crooks, the crippled Negro stable boy, tells them he will work for free if they will take him in too. Curley accuses George of pursuing his wife, and in the ensuing fight, Lennie crushes Curley's hand.

Act III:

While Lennie mourns over a puppy he has accidentally killed, Curley's wife comes into the barn. She invites Lennie to stroke her hair, but then becomes frightened. Lennie, attempting to quiet her screams, snaps her neck and then runs away. George finds Lennie, and while distracting him with talk of the farm that will soon be theirs, shoots him in the head before Curley's lynch mob can reach him.

Theatre History and Popular Response:

Of Mice and Men opened at the Music Box on Novem-

ber 23, 1937, and ran for 207 performances. The event
marked Steinbeck's first appearance as a dramatist, and the
play became the talk of the town overnight. The reviews
were laudatory, and with less formidable competition than
Our Town the play might have won the Pulitzer Prize as
well as the Circle Award. But as John Toohey expressed
it (A History of The Pulitzer Prize Plays, 1967), "unfortunately, its earthiness was forced to compete with a com-
bination of spirituality, nostalgia and novelty." For representative reviews, see: Literary Digest, December 18, 1937,
p. 34; Nation, December 11, 1937, pp. 663-664; Scribner's,
February, 1938, p. 70; Theatre Arts, October, 1937, pp.
774-81.

Critical Reputation:

        John Steinbeck (1902-1968), was born in Salinas, Cali-
fornia, and educated in the public schools and Stanford University. Although he wrote several plays--The Moon is
Down (1942), Burning Bright (1950), and Pipe Dream (1955),
a musical comedy based on his novel Sweet Thursday (1954)--
he is established in the history of American literature as a
novelist rather than a dramatist. Consequently, there has
been little scholarly interest in his plays. For a basic guide
to Steinbeck studies, see Steinbeck and His Critics: A Record
of Twenty-Five Years, 1957, by E. W. Tatlock and C. V.
Wicker. An early but still valuable source of biographical
and bibliographical information is Harry T. Moore's The
Novels of John Steinbeck, 1939. The most scholarly treatment of Steinbeck's works to date is Peter Lisca's The Wide
World of John Steinbeck, 1958. For a good general introduction, see Warren French's John Steinbeck, 1961. A discussion of the play Of Mice and Men can be found in Lisca's
book, pp. 130-143. See also John Mason Brown's Two On
the Aisle, 1938, pp. 183-187; and Joseph Wood Krutch's
American Drama Since 1918, 1957, pp. 73-133.

The Theatre Season of

1938-1939

The Pulitzer Prize this season went to Robert E. Sherwood's Abe Lincoln in Illinois. The Critic's Circle Award was not given this season, not because there were no deserving plays in the critics' opinion, but because the competition was keen and no play received the number of votes necessary to win. The choice was among The Little Foxes, My Heart's in the Highlands, Rocket to the Moon, The Philadelphia Story, The American Way, No Time for Comedy, and the Pulitzer winner Abe Lincoln in Illinois.

ABE LINCOLN IN ILLINOIS

Characters:

Mentor Graham	Trum Cogdal
Abe Lincoln	Jack Armstrong
Ann Rutledge	Bab
Judith	Feargus
Ben Mattling	Jasp
Judge Bowling Green	Seth Gale
Ninian Edwards	Nancy Green
Joshua Speed	William Herndon
Elizabeth Edwards	The Lincolns' Maid
Mary Todd	Crimmin
The Edwards' Maid	Barrick
Jimmy Gale	Sturveson
Aggie Gale	Jed
Gobey	Phil
Stephen A. Douglas	Kavanagh
Willie Lincoln	Ogleby
Tad Lincoln	Donner
Robert Lincoln	Cavalry Captain

Act I:

In New Salem, Illinois, during the 1830's, the young

69

Abe Lincoln busies himself with his studies and makes many friends, in spite of his curious misanthropic streak. When his friend, Judge Bowling Green, and the Governor's son, Ninian Edwards, suggest that he run for the state assembly, Abe remains unconvinced that he is the man for the job until Ann Rutledge declares her affection for him. Encouraged by her faith in him, he agrees to enter politics, but her untimely death plunges him into despair.

Act II:

Abe, now 31, has opened a law office in Springfield, but his political career seems at a standstill, due, in part, to his inability to commit himself to any cause. Ninian Edwards' sister-in-law, Mary Todd, however, sees in Abe a man of enormous potential and proclaims her intention to marry him and shape his destiny. Abe, on the verge of a nervous collapse, jilts her on their wedding day and goes back to New Salem, where he meets an old friend trying to take his family West for a new start. Suddenly, Abe has a vision of America as a stronghold of freedom, and he accepts the preservation of this concept as his destiny. He and Mary are reconciled, and he decides to seek public office again.

Act III:

By 1858, Abe, now a candidate for State Senator from Illinois, furthers his reputation by participating in the famous debates with Stephen Douglas, and in 1860, the party considers him a possible candidate for President. Secretly, they believe him an infidel and a rabble rouser, but they are confident he can get votes.

On election eve, when Abe's victory looks doubtful, the neurotic Mary turns on him an attack of such shattering fury that his subsequent triumph seems hollow.

In 1861, as President and Mrs. Lincoln board the train for Washington, Abe tells the assembled crowd that the union must be saved, for if it perishes, men's ancient dream of liberty will perish with it.

History and Reviews:

Abe Lincoln in Illinois opened at the Plymouth Thea-

tre on October 15, 1938, and ran for 472 performances.
Many critics found it a poignant and impressive play, but
others complained that it was too episodic, tried to cover
too much material, and depended too heavily on the audience's predictable response to a great folk hero.   Still, the
play probably had more admirers than detractors.   For representative reviews, see: Catholic World, December, 1938,
pp. 340-341; Forum, February, 1939, p. 72; Newsweek,
October 31, 1938, p. 29; Theatre Arts, December, 1938,
pp. 853-855.

Critical Reputation:

        For an introduction to Sherwood's life and works,
consult the entry for 1935-1936.   Discussions of Abe Lincoln
in Illinois can be found in the critical studies noted there.

The Theatre Season of

1939-1940

William Saroyan won the Pulitzer Prize this season
for his play The Time of Your Life. He declined to accept
the award, however, and returned the $1,000 check, the
only drama winner in Pulitzer Prize history ever to do so.
(Sinclair Lewis, earlier, had refused the award for fiction.)
Another "first" occurred this season--the critics and the
Pulitzer Prize committee agreed for the first time, and
The Time of Your Life won the Circle Award as well. Other
contenders were Life with Father, The Male Animal, The
Man Who Came To Dinner, and Mornings at Seven.

THE TIME OF YOUR LIFE

Characters:

Joe	Krupp
Tom	Harry
Kitty Duval	Wesley
Nick	Dudley
Arab	Elsie
Kit Carson	Lorene
McCarthy	Mary L.
Willie	A Sailor
Blick	A Society Gentleman
Ma	A Society Lady
A Killer	The Drunkard
Her Side Kick	The Newsboy
A Cop	Anna
Another Cop	

Act I:

The habitues of Nick's Pacific Street Saloon in San
Francisco include Joe, a young man who is trying to find a
way to live without hurting anyone; Tom, his rather simple-

72

minded friend, who has fallen in love with Kitty Duval, a
prostitute who longs for a better life; Wesley, a Negro piano
player; McCarthy, an intellectual longshoreman; Willie, a
slot-machine enthusiast; The Arab, a melancholy philosopher;
and Kit Carson, an old Indian fighter who regales the group
with tales of his career. The cozy atmosphere of the saloon
is shattered with the appearance of Blick, a sadistic detective, who threatens to return and shut the place down.

Act II:

Joe, hoping to provide Tom with the means to marry
Kitty and take her off the streets, gives him some money to
bet on a horse, but Joe arrives one minute late to place the
bet and loses $5,000.

Act III:

Joe goes with Tom to Kitty's room to comfort her,
but to their dismay, Kitty's clients keep knocking on the
door and calling for her.

Act IV:

The barroom philosophers gather. Elsie Mandelspiegel
tells her sweetheart, Dudley, that love in this world is impossible; Krupp, a young policeman, describes his disgust
with the world; the Arab gloomily asserts that nothing has
any foundation.

Act V:

Joe, who has arranged for Kitty to move to a respectable hotel, also arranges for Tom to get a job, for he knows
that Kitty could not survive without Tom. Blick returns and
begins abusing Kitty; when Kit Carson protests, Blick beats
him up, whereupon Kit, with everyone's approval, shoots him.
Meanwhile, Joe has hustled Kitty and Tom off to be married.

History and Reviews:

The Time of Your Life opened at the Booth Theatre
on October 25, 1939, and ran for 185 performances. The
critics murmured about its sprawling formlessness but, unable
to resist its originality, vigor, and poignancy, pronounced it
enchanting--"an honor to American dramatic writing." For

representative reviews, see: New Republic, November 29, 1939, p. 169; New Yorker, October 23, 1939, p. 130; Theatre Arts, January, 1940, pp. 11-13; Time, November 6, 1939, p. 22.

Critical Reputation:

       William Saroyan (1908-   ), born of Armenian parents in Fresno, California, had little formal education but began reading and writing stories at an early age. He began his literary career in 1933 with the publication of a volume of short stories entitled The Daring Young Man on the Flying Trapeze. Although Saroyan was excoriated by critics who deplored his eccentric and highly subjective style, the book became a best seller. In 1939 he made his debut as a playwright with My Heart's in the Highlands. Since that time he has written, produced and directed many plays and has done screenplays and television scripts. Some of his best known plays are: The Beautiful People (1941), Hello Out There (1945), and The Cave Dwellers (1957). Although critics still argue about the literary merit of his works, he has proved an enduring favorite with American audiences, not at all the "flash in the pan" that he was predicted to be. For further information about his life and work, see The Biographical Encyclopedia and Who's Who of the American Theatre, 1966. Howard R. Floan's William Saroyan, 1966, is a book-length study of his work. A shorter work which discusses Saroyan's place in American Literature is Frederick I. Carpenter's "The Time of William Saroyan's Life, " Pacific Spectator, I (1947), 88-96. Another useful discussion can be found in John Gassner's The Theatre in Our Time, 1954, 297-302. For discussion of The Time of Your Life, consult J. M. Brown's Broadway in Review, 1940, pp. 189-194; Winifred Dusenbury's Theme of Loneliness in Modern American Drama, 1960, pp. 155-178; and Mary McCarthy's Sights and Spectacles, 1961, pp. 46-52.

The Theatre Season of

1940-1941

This season Robert E. Sherwood won his third Pulitzer Prize for Drama. His play, There Shall Be No Night, concerned the embattled Finns on the eve of the Soviet invasion. Lillian Hellman's anti-Fascist play Watch On The Rhine took the Drama Critics' Circle Award. Also running were Native Son, Lady in the Dark and Claudia.

THERE SHALL BE NO NIGHT

Characters:

Dr. Kaarlo Valkonen   Joe Burnett
Miranda Valkonen   Ben Gichner
Dave Corween   Frank Olmstead
Uncle Waldemar   Sergeant Gosden
Gus Shuman   Lempi
Erik Valkonen   Ilma
Kaatri Alquist   Photographer
Dr. Ziemssen   Photographer
Major Rutkowski

Scene I:

As the war clouds gather over Europe in 1938, Dr. Kaarlo Valkonen, a Finnish neurologist of international reputation and a recent recipient of the Nobel prize, broadcasts a speech to America deploring the barbarism of the Hitler regime.

Scene II:

In the face of the Soviet invasion of Finland the following year, Kaarlo, an ardent pacifist, is distressed because his son, Erik, and Erik's fiancee, Kaatri, insist they will fight.

Scene III:

The next day, Erik leaves for the north to join the ski troops. Kaarlo tries in vain to persuade his charming wife, Miranda, an American, to leave for the States before it is too late.

Scene IV:

As Kaarlo prepares to leave for the front to join the medical corps, Kaatri arrives and announces that she is pregnant. She insists she will not bring a baby into a war-torn world, but both Kaarlo and Miranda convince her to bear the child.

Scene V:

After Erik is killed, Miranda arranges to send Kaatri to the United States to bear the child.

Scene VI:

Kaarlo learns of Erik's death just as the Russians are closing in. He tears off his Red Cross arm band, straps on a revolver, and prepares to advance on the enemy.

Scene VII:

In Helsinki, after hearing of Kaarlo's death, Miranda and Kaarlo's Uncle Waldemar calmly await the siege of the city. In keeping with the Finnish policy of resisting to the last man, Miranda and Waldemar plan to set fire to the house and make a last gallant stand in the garden.

History and Reviews:

There Shall Be No Night was first presented at The Alvin Theatre in April 29, 1940, and ran for 115 perform-ances. Many of the critics, moved by Sherwood's obvious conviction and impressed by the luminous performances of Alfred Lunt and Lynn Fontanne, praised the play, although they complained of its faulty structure. Many echoed George Jean Nathan's observation that though the play was "brave in intent" and "thoroughly high-minded," as a drama it was "defective, inconclusive and inert." For representative re-views, see: Nation, May 11, 1940, pp. 605-606; New Yorker,

May 11, 1940, p. 28; Theatre Arts, June, 1940, pp. 398-
401; Time, May 13, 1940, p. 52.

Critical Reputation:

    For a general introduction to Sherwood's life and art
see the entry for 1935-1936. For discussions of There Shall
Be No Night see the critical studies noted here.

WATCH ON THE RHINE

Characters:

        Anise   Sara Muller
        Joseph   Joshua Muller
        Fanny Farrelly   Bodo Muller
        David Farrelly   Babette Muller
        Marthe De Brancovis   Kurt Muller
        Teck De Brancovis

Act I:

    In the spring of 1940, Fanny Farrelly, widow of an
American diplomat, awaits the arrival of her daughter, Sara,
who has lived abroad since her marriage to Kurt Muller, a
German engineer, some twenty years before. Meanwhile,
an impoverished Roumanian count, Teck de Brancovis, and
his wife, Marthe, are imposing on her hospitality. Marthe
spends her time running up bills and flirting with Fanny's
son David, while Teck plays cards with Nazis at the German
embassy. When Sara and her family arrive, Fanny is appalled at their threadbare appearance. While the families
greet each other Teck secretly examines Kurt's luggage.

Act II:

    When Kurt, an anti-fascist agent, learns that three
of his fellow agents have been captured and imprisoned by
the Nazis, he knows he must return to Germany to bargain
for their release with the $23,000 he has collected for anti-
fascist causes. Teck threatens to report him to the Nazis
unless he pays him $10,000. Marthe, repelled by such tac-
tics, announces that she is leaving Teck for good, in the
hopes of making a match with David.

Act III:

   Kurt refuses to spend any of the money to keep Teck
quiet about his mission. Fanny offers to put up the money,
but Kurt, unwilling to trust Teck, kills him instead. Fanny,
horrified at first, finally sees the justice of his cause, promises to cover up the murder until he is out of the country,
and gives him $10,000 for his work. After a touching fare-
well with Sara and the children, Kurt leaves, promising to
do his best to return.

Theatre History and Popular Response:

   Watch on the Rhine opened on April 1, 1941, at the
Martin Beck Theatre and ran for 378 performances. Generally, the critics praised it as a moving and beautiful play,
though some observed that it lacked the tightness of structure exhibited by Hellman's earlier work. Its flaws were
nevertheless considered minor technicalities, and most of
the reviewers received the play enthusiastically. For representative reviews, see Catholic World, May, 1941, pp.
215-216; New Republic, April 14, 1941, pp. 498-499; Theatre Arts, June, 1941, pp. 409-411; Time, April 14, 1941,
p. 64.

Critical Reputation:

   Lillian Hellman (1905-) was born in New Orleans,
Louisiana, but spent time in New York, where her father's
business interests kept him part of each year. She attended
public schools, then did work at New York University and
Columbia. She worked for a time for a publishing company
and later as promotion and subscription manager for a stock
company. Her first play, The Children's Hour (1934),
missed getting the Pulitzer Prize because of its lesbian
theme, but it established her as a playwright of merit.
Since then, she has won the Circle Award twice--once for
Watch on the Rhine and again for Toys in the Attic (1959-
1960). She has never, however, been awarded a Pulitzer
Prize. For a recent book-length study of her art, see
Jacob E. Adler's Lillian Hellman, (1969). Other useful discussions of her work can be found in the major studies of
American drama. See, for example, John Gassner's Thea-
tre at the Crossroads, 1960, pp. 132-139, and Allen Lewis'
American Plays and Playwrights of the Contemporary Thea-

tre, 1965, pp. 99-116.

The Theatre Season of

1941-1942

Neither the Pulitzer Prize nor the Circle Award was given this season. Technically, Lillian Hellman's Watch on the Rhine was eligible for the Pulitzer since it opened on April 1, 1941, and was considered by the Pulitzer Committee a play of the 1941-42 season. (The New York Drama Critics considered it a 1940-41 play and gave it the Circle Award for that period.) Also passed over were In Time to Come, The Moon Is Down, Junior Miss, Candle in the Wind, and The Land Is Bright.

The Theatre Season of

1942-1943

The Pulitzer Prize this season went to Thornton
Wilder's fantasy, The Skin of Our Teeth. According to John
Toohey (A History of the Pulitzer Prize Plays, 1967), the
drama critics were prepared to give the play the Circle
Award but hedged because Wilder was accused of having
taken much of the material from James Joyce's Finnegans
Wake. They chose instead Sidney Kingsley's historical play,
The Patriots.

THE SKIN OF OUR TEETH

Characters:

Announcer	Doctor
Sabina	Professor
Mrs. Fitzpatrick	Judge
Mrs. Antrobus	Homer
Dinosaur	Miss E. Muse
Mammoth	Miss T. Muse
Telegraph Boy	Miss M. Muse
Gladys	Usher
Henry	Usher
Mr. Antrobus	Girl
Girl	Conveener
Fortune Teller	Broadcast Official
Chair Pusher	Defeated Candidate
Chair Pusher	Mr. Tremayne
Conveener	Hester
Conveener	Ivy
Conveener	Fred Bailey
Conveener	Drum Majorettes

Act I:

During the Ice Age, the Antrobus household--George
and his wife, his children Henry and Gladys, and their faith-

ful servant Lily Sabina--struggle gallantly to surmount the
many hardships presented by life in this difficult time.   At
first they do rather well; George, for example, invents the
wheel and the alphabet, discovers the number 100 and in the
face of an approaching glacier, manages to build an enormous
fire and keep it going.   Mr. Antrobus is confident that man
will prevail, but he suffers a setback when his son Henry
kills the boy next door.   When the despondent George loses
interest in the fire, Mrs. Antrobus convinces him that they
have survived too much to give up now.

Act II:

     At a convention in Atlantic City, George is elected
president of the Order of Mammals, Subdivision Humans.
He and Mrs. Antrobus are celebrating their five-thousandth
wedding anniversary, but when Sabina, now Lily-Sabina Fair-
weather, a beauty contest winner, makes a play for him he
allows himself to be seduced and even promises to marry
her.   His amours are interrupted by the Flood, an event
predicted by an old fortune teller, who advises Antrobus to
gather his family and a pair of each of the animals into a
boat. Antrobus follows the advice.

Act III:

     At the end of a shattering war, Sabina, now a camp
follower, arrives at the Antrobus house to find Mrs. Antrobus and Gladys, who now has a baby.   Henry, a confirmed
enemy of his father, appears and threatens to kill him.   Father and son quarrel bitterly, but Sabina manages to bring
them to terms.   Mr. Antrobus, surveying the ruins of his
world, confides to his wife that he has no desire to build
and plan again, but Mrs. Antrobus infuses him with courage
to begin anew.   Sabina appears and recites the opening lines
of the play, then advises the audience to go home as the
play will go on for ages.

Theatre History and Popular Response:

     The Skin of Our Teeth opened on November 18, 1942
at the Plymouth Theatre and ran for 359 performances.   Although the play proved popular, neither critics nor public
knew quite what to make of it.   The reviewers agreed, generally, that the play was amusing, inventive, and provocative,
but some found it superficial, a mere prank or stunt show

with a funnypaper quality which finally wearied. For representative reviews, see: Commonweal, December 4, 1942,
pp. 175-176; New Yorker, November 28, 1942, p. 35; Newsweek, November 30, 1942, p. 86; Time, November 30, 1942,
p. 57.

Critical Reputation:

     For a general introduction to Wilder's life and work,
see the entry for 1937-1938. For an understanding of the
Skin of our Teeth-Finnegans Wake controversy, see the ac-
cusation by Joseph Campbell and H. M. Robinson in Saturday Review, December 19, 1942, pp. 3-4; and February 13,
1943, pp. 16-19. Edmund Wilson's assessment of the problem appears in his article "The Antrobuses and the Ear-
wickers, " The Nation, January 30, 1943, pp. 167-168. For
critical analyses of the play, consult the studies of Wilder's
art listed above. See also Robert Corrigan's "Thornton
Wilder and the Tragic Sense of Life, " Educational Theatre
Journal, XIII (1961), 167-73; Francis Fergusson's "Three
Allegorists: Brecht, Wilder and Eliot, " Sewanee Review,
LXIV (1956), 544-73; Edmund Wilson's Classics and Com-
mercials: A Literary Chronicle of the Forties, 1952, pp. 81-
86.

THE PATRIOTS

Characters:

Captain	James Monroe
Thomas Jefferson	Mrs. Hamilton
Patsy	Henry Knox
Martha	Butler
James Madison	Mr. Fenno
Alexander Hamilton	Jupiter
George Washington	Mrs. Conrad
Sergeant	Frontierman
Colonel Humphreys	Thomas Jefferson Randolph
Jacob	Anne Randolph
Ned	George Washington Lafayette
Mat	

Prologue:

     After an absence of six years, Thomas Jefferson,
weary, still grieving over the death of his wife, and longing

to take up the life of gentleman farmer at Monticello, returns to the United States from France.

Act I:

     Jefferson returns to find the country near anarchy,
and when Washington begs him to become Secretary of State,
he cannot refuse. He meets Alexander Hamilton who tries
to enlist his support for his money bill, now before Congress,
which would pay one hundred cents on the dollar for all money issued by the States, a measure Hamilton insists will re-
store order to the country's chaotic financial affairs. Jefferson agrees to study the bill; then he and Washington, two
weary men longing for home, steal away to go fishing.

Act II:

     After Hamilton's money bill passes, it becomes ap-
parent that many people have lost their savings to specula-
tors. Furthermore, Hamilton himself is accused of having
speculated with public funds, a charge he later denies,
though he confesses he has been blackmailed for philander-
ing. The conflict between Hamilton and Jefferson intensifies.
Hamilton fears and distrusts the common man and blames
Jefferson for the revolutionary fever sweeping the country.
Jefferson abhors Hamilton's aristocratic philosophy and vows
to fight him in order to create a truly democratic society.

Act III:

     Although Jefferson has been elected President by popu-
lar vote, the Congress is deadlocked by a group which wants
to set his election aside. Hamilton promises to deliver the
Presidency to Jefferson in return for some concessions later,
a bargain Jefferson emphatically rejects. When he explains
to Hamilton that the people's desire for freedom is stronger
than any scheme or any tyrant, Hamilton, awed by Jefferson's faith in the people, agrees to secure his election anyway. The play ends with Jefferson's inaugural address.

Theatre History and Popular Response:

     The Patriots, which opened at the National Theatre
on January 29, 1943, ran for 157 performances. The play
was not enthusiastically received by the critics who complained of its unsteady beginning, flat ending, wooden char-

acterizations and stiff, literary dialogue. Still, they conceded that the "material triumphed over the defects of the writing," and that the play rose at times to eloquence. For representative reviews, see: American Mercury, April, 1943, pp. 486-487; Commonweal, February 12, 1943, p. 422; New Yorker, February 6, 1943, p. 31; Theatre Arts, April, 1943, pp. 201-204.

Critical Reputation:

For an introduction to Sidney Kingsley's life and work, see the entry for 1933-1934. For discussions of The Patriots see S. Shirk's Characterizations of George Washington in American Drama Since 1875, 1949, 77-81; and John Gassner's "Jefferson and Hamilton in Drama," Current History, IV (1943), 88-91.

The Theatre Season of

1943-1944

Neither the Pulitzer Prize nor the Circle Award was given this season. Passed by were Winged Victory, The Searching Wind, and Oklahoma!

The Theatre Season of

1944-1945

This season the Pulitzer Prize went to Harvey by
Mary Chase, a controversial selection in view of the fact
that Tennessee Williams' The Glass Menagerie, the critics'
choice, was eligible. Other contenders were A Bell for
Adano, The Late George Apley, Anna Lucasta, I Remember
Mama and Soldier's Wife.

HARVEY

Characters:

Myrtle Mae Simmons	Lyman Sanderson, M.D.
Veta Louise Simmons	William H. Chumley, M.D.
Elwood P. Dowd	Betty Chumley
Miss Johnson	Judge Omar Gaffney
Mrs. Ethel Chauvenet	E. J. Lofgren
Ruth Kelly, R.N.	

Act I:

To the dismay of his sister, Veta Simmons, Elwood
P. Dowd, usually a bit tipsy, claims to have as his insepa-
rable companion a huge white rabbit named Harvey. Although Harvey is invisible to nearly everyone else--Mrs.
Simmons has only caught a glimpse of him--Elwood persists
in buying him theatre tickets, setting his place at table, and
introducing him to everyone he meets.

Veta, impatient with her boozy brother's eccentricity,
which she fears will hurt her daughter Myrtle Mae's chances
of catching a husband, decides to have her brother committed
to a sanatorium, Chumley's Rest. When she describes her
brother's problem to Dr. Sanderson, the doctor in charge,
he assumes that she is the crazy one and locks her up. By
the time he realizes his mistake, Elwood has gone, and Dr.
Chumley sets out to look for him.

Act II:

  Upon returning home, Mrs. Simmons, furious about
the treatment she received at Chumley's Rest, tells Judge
Gaffney that she intends to sue. Meanwhile, at the hospital
Dr. Sanderson and the other attendants anxiously await word
from Dr. Chumley, who is still chasing Elwood, whom they
assume to be dangerous. Elwood arrives, however, and re-
ports that Dr. Chumley and Harvey, now fast friends, are
still touring the bars together. When Chumley finally appears, he seems shaken and insists he is being followed,
presumably by Harvey.

Act III:

  Dr. Chumley, who now wants Harvey for himself because the rabbit can predict the future and make time stand
still, encourages Elwood to have an injection which will
bring him back to reality. Because Veta and Myrtle insist
upon it, Elwood agrees, but just as he is about to receive
the shot, a taxi driver appears and tells Veta how sad the
patients are after they have been treated. She calls a halt
to the procedure, declaring that she prefers Elwood the way
he is. Harvey arrives about this time, and they all leave
together.

Theatre History and Popular Response:

  Harvey, which opened at the 48th Street Theatre on
November 1, 1944, ran for over four years, 1,775 performances in all. Most of the critics found it a charming
play, so full of fun and so fresh that its structural defects
passed unnoticed. A dissenter complained that the play was
"a slipshod farce" whose stock characters had been "hacked
rather crudely out of a very low grade of theatrical card-
board." For representative reviews, see: Life, November
27, 1944, pp. 96-98; Nation, November 18, 1944, p. 624;
New Yorker, November 11, 1944, p. 44; Newsweek, November 13, 1944, 82-83.

Critical Reputation:

  Mary Coyle Chase (1907-) was born in Denver,
Colorado, attended public schools, and then studied at the
University of Denver and the University of Colorado. She

left school for a job as a newspaper reporter. She got the
idea for Harvey from stories her Irish relatives told about
"pookas," which were, according to Celtic mythology, spirits
of large animals visible only to certain people. Two of Ms.
Chase's later plays, Mrs. McThing (1952) and Bernadine
(1953) had successful Broadway runs but were not as popular
as Harvey. For details of Miss Chase's life, consult Current Biography, 1945. For discussions of Harvey, see Ivor
Brown and Athene Seyler's "Harvey," World Review, April,
1949, pp. 17-20; John Mason Brown's Seeing Things, 1946,
pp. 212-216; Lillian Hornstein's "Harvey: Or Sanity in the
Theatre," College English, VIII (October, 1946), 37-38;
Gerard Larson's "From Ten Nights to Harvey: Drinking on
the American Stage," Western Humanities Review, X (1956),
390; and Jordan Miller's American Dramatic Literature,
1961, pp. 467-469.

THE GLASS MENAGERIE

Characters:

      Amanda Wingfield   Tom Wingfield
      Laura Wingfield   Jim O'Connor

Part I

Scene I:

    As the curtain rises, Tom Wingfield appears and ex-
plains that the play is his memory. Then, as the interior
of a tenement apartment becomes visible, Amanda Wingfield
enters, calling her children, Tom and Laura, to the table.
She exhorts Laura to stay fresh and pretty for her gentlemen
callers. When Laura insists she isn't expecting any, Amanda
launches into a story of how she once, as the reigning belle
of Blue Mountain, received seventeen gentlemen callers in
one afternoon. Then, looking at the picture of the husband
who deserted her many years before, she confesses that she
chose foolishly.

Scene II:

    Amanda comes home in a rage after discovering that
Laura has stopped going to business school. When Laura
confesses that she never had the courage to return after the
first day, Amanda tries to convince her she cannot spend the

rest of her life at home, playing with her collection of glass
animals. She must forget her affliction (Laura is slightly
crippled), overcome her shyness, and get herself a husband.
Laura confesses that she was once interested in Jim O'Connor, a boy she knew in high school, but he scarcely paid any
attention to her.

Scene III:

Tom and Amanda quarrel violently. She accuses him
of selfishness, but he insists that if he were really selfish
he would desert her and Laura just as his father did.

Scene IV:

The next day, Tom and Amanda make up. Amanda
knows he longs to escape, but she pleads with him to find a
husband for Laura before he goes. He agrees to look for
someone suitable.

Scene V:

Several days later, Tom announces that a friend, Jim
O'Connor, is coming to dinner the next evening. Amanda
begins making feverish plans to fix up the apartment and to
get Laura a new dress. Tom, reminding Amanda that outsiders are likely to consider Laura a bit peculiar, begs her
not to expect too much.

Part II

Scene VI:

Tom, as narrator, describes Jim as a nice boy but
one who has not lived up to his promise. When Laura realizes the caller is the same Jim she admired in high school,
she flees in a fit of nervousness. Amanda carries on alone,
exuding flirtatious Southern charm.

Scene VII:

After the meal, Tom helps Amanda while Jim makes
a point of being nice to Laura. Laura, encouraged by Jim's
kindness, overcomes some of her shyness. After waltzing
her around the room, Jim kisses her, then hastens to apolo-
gize, declaring that he had no right to the kiss because he is
engaged. After Jim leaves, Amanda, her hopes dashed, flies

into a rage at Tom, who threatens to leave them for good.

Tom appears again in the role of narrator and explains that he did leave home, but since that time he has wandered like one pursued, unable to put the haunting memory of his sister out of his mind.

Theatre History and Popular Response:

The Glass Menagerie opened at the Playhouse on March 31, 1945 and ran for 561 performances. The critics were overwhelmed. Only the strict perfectionists observed that perhaps the play had some flaws; for the rest, the play was "fragile and poignant," "enchanting," and "something to cheer about." Its eerie beauty prompted one to say that the play hurt him through and through. For representative reviews, see: Catholic World, May, 1945, pp. 166-167; Life, April 30, 1945, pp. 81-83; Nation, April 14, 1945, p. 424; New Republic, April 16, 1945, p. 505; Theatre Arts, June, 1945, pp. 325-327.

Critical Reception:

Tennessee (Thomas Lanier) Williams (1921-   ), was born in Columbus, Mississippi, the son of a travelling shoe salesman. He grew up in St. Louis, Missouri, attended the University of Missouri, and finally took his degree from the University of Iowa (B.A., 1938). He won prizes for prose, poetry and plays almost from the time he started to write, but with The Glass Menagerie he moved into the front rank of American playwrights. A steadily prolific writer, he has won the Pulitzer Prize twice and the Circle Award four times. The amount of criticism his work has attracted is vast; for bibliographical guides, see Nadine Dony's "Tennessee Williams: A Selected Bibliography," Modern Drama, I (1958), 181-191; and Charles Carpenter and Elizabeth Cook's "Addenda to 'Tennessee Williams, A Selected Bibliography'," Modern Drama, II (1959), 220-223. Gerald Weales' Tennessee Williams, 1965, provides a brief introduction to his work; longer critical studies are: Signi Falk's Tennessee Williams, 1961; Benjamin Nelson's Tennessee Williams: The Man and His Work, 1961; Nancy Tischler's Tennessee Williams: Rebellious Puritan, 1961; Francis Donahue's The Dramatic World of Tennessee Williams, 1964; and Esther Jackson's The Broken World of Tennessee Williams, 1965.

For critical articles on The Glass Menagerie see: Lester
Beaurline's "The Glass Menagerie: From Story to Play, "
Modern Drama, VIII (1965), pp. 142-149; Sam Bluefarb,
"The Glass Menagerie: Three Visions of Time, " College
English, XXIV (1963), 513-518; Paul T. Nolan's "Two Mem-
ory Plays: The Glass Menagerie and After the Fall, " Mc-
Neese Review, XVII (1966), 27-38; Roger Stein's "The Glass
Menagerie Revisited: Catastrophe Without Violence, " Western
Humanities Review, XVIII (Spring, 1964), 141-153.

The Theatre Season of

1945-1946

The Pulitzer Prize went this season to State of the
Union, a political comedy by Howard Lindsay and Russel
Crouse. The drama critics gave no Best Play award, pass-
ing up Home of the Brave, The Magnificent Yankee, Deep
are the Roots, Born Yesterday, and Dream Girl, as well as
State of the Union.

STATE OF THE UNION

Characters:

James Conover	Sam Parrish
Spike McManus	Swenson
Kay Thorndyke	Judge Jefferson Davis Alexander
Grant Matthews	Mrs. Alexander
Norah	Jennie
Mary Matthews	Mrs. Draper
Stevens	William Hardy
Bellboy	Senator Lauterback
Waiter	

Act I:

Republican party boss Jim Conover considers Grant
Matthews, a tycoon who has never before been in politics,
good Presidential material. He discovers, however, that
Matthews is given to speaking his mind rather too freely for
a political hopeful; furthermore, Matthews is having an affair with Kay Thorndyke, a newspaper publisher, and the
relationship may prove difficult to conceal. Conover, hoping
to quell rumors, sends Matthews and his wife Mary on a
speaking tour across the country. Mary realizes that Conover
is using her to further Grant's career, but because she believes her husband would be a good President, she agrees to
go along.

91

Act II:

    While on the trip, Grant speaks forcefully and direct-
ly to a number of groups, with Mary's encouragement. Although his popularity at the grassroots grows, Conover, dismayed by Matthews' political naivete, warns him that the pol-
iticians, not the people, elect the President. Matthews equiv-
ocates only once, in Detroit, after Jim sneaks in Kay Thorndyke to talk to him.

Act III:

    At the Matthews' New York apartment, Mary and
Grant give a dinner party for a group of important politicos.
When Mary, already disgusted with the compromises a successful politician must make, learns that Kay Thorndyke
talked Grant into modifying his speech in Detroit, she drinks
a bit too much and speaks her mind about corruption in
American political life. Grant, suddenly realizing the wisdom in Mary's point of view, declares that in order to give
the country his vision of American life, he will not be a
candidate for President. The play implies that Mary has
won Grant back, and that the party will probably accept
Grant on his own terms.

Theatre History and Popular Response:

    State of the Union, which opened at the Hudson Thea-
tre on November 14, 1945, proved exceptionally popular and
ran for 765 performances. The reviewers, while not overcome by the play, agreed that Lindsay and Crouse had come
up with a good show. With wit and sentiment, it had something to say and said it. That the play dragged in spots
seemed hardly worth mentioning. For representative reviews, see: Forum, January, 1946, pp. 466-468; Life, December 10, 1945, pp. 85-86; New Republic, November 26,
1945, p. 711.

Critical Reputation:

    Russel Crouse (1893-1966), born in Findlay, Ohio, and
educated in the public schools, began his career as a newspaperman in Cincinnati, Kansas City and New York. Lured
by the theatre, he started writing plays. In 1934 he met
Howard Lindsay, and together they produced some of the

most successful of American comedies. Lindsay (1889-
1968), born at Waterford, New York, spent a year at Harvard, then worked in the theatre acting, writing, and staging
plays. Some of the plays that Crouse and Lindsay wrote together were Life with Father (1939), Arsenic and Old Lace
(1940), and Call Me Madam (1950). The major studies of
the American theatre devote space to the phenomenally successful team, but their work has not been the subject of
much serious scholarly investigation. For a discussion of
State of the Union, see George Jean Nathan's Theatre Book
of the Year, 1945-1946, pp. 184-186. For a biographical
sketch of both Crouse and Lindsay, consult Biographical Encyclopedia and Who's Who of the American Theatre, 1966.

The Theatre Season of

1946-1947

The Pulitzer Prize Committee gave no award during
this exciting theatre season. The Circle Award went to
Arthur Miller's All My Sons, his second Broadway play.
Passed over were: The Iceman Cometh and Another Part
of the Forest.

ALL MY SONS

Characters:

Joe Keller	Sue Bayliss
Kate Keller	Frank Lubey
Chris Keller	Lydie Lubey
Ann Deever	Bert
George Deever	Dr. Jim Bayliss

Act I:

In the first few scenes of the play, Joe Keller and
his wife Kate appear to be a normal middle-class couple
whose only problem is that their oldest son, Larry, reported
missing in action during the war three years before, has
never returned. Trouble begins, however, when Chris,
their youngest son, reveals his plans to marry Larry's
former sweetheart, Ann, who is now paying them a visit.
Kate will not hear of the match, for she cannot admit that
Larry is dead. Her insistence that he is still alive stems
from the fact that during the war, Joe and Ann's father,
former business partners, had manufactured and shipped
some defective cylinder heads, causing the death of some
American fliers. Kate cannot face the fact that Larry could
have been one of these pilots. Because Ann's father is still
serving a prison term and claims to have taken the rap for
Joe, who was exonerated, Joe fears the girl has come to
stir up the old scandal and perhaps reopen the case. He is

94

especially disturbed because George, Ann's brother, now a
lawyer, is about to arrive, claiming to have urgent business
with Ann.

Act II:

Joe's nervousness increases when George appears and
says he has heard from his father's own mouth that Joe ordered him to patch up the defective cylinder heads and ship
them out. Keller almost succeeds in convincing him otherwise when Kate makes a slip of the tongue, confirming Keller's guilt. In a shattering scene, Chris forces his father
to confess that he alone was responsible.

Act III:

Chris wants his father to give himself up and serve
a prison term to pay for his crime. Joe defends himself by
insisting that he sent out the parts to save the business for
Chris. Chris, an idealist, refuses to accept this excuse,
insisting that a man has higher loyalties than those to his
family. Joe claims that Larry would have understood and
forgiven him, but when Ann produces a letter from Larry,
in which he condemns his father's act and says he plans to
commit suicide by crashing his plane, Joe goes upstairs and
shoots himself.

Theatre History and Popular Response:

All My Sons opened at the Coronet Theatre on January 29, 1947, and ran for 328 performances. With this
play, Miller was proclaimed a promising new talent. Although the reviewers took note of the play's defects--its un-
evenness, its melodramatic plot, its occasional failure to
convince--they agreed that Miller had written a play of
"extraordinary poignancy and power." For representative
reviews, see: Commonweal, February 14, 1947, pp. 445-
446; Nation, February 15, 1947, p. 191; Saturday Review,
March 1, 1947, pp. 22-24; Theatre Arts, April, 1947, p.
19, 50.

Critical Reputation:

Arthur Miller (1915-   ) was born into a New York
family whose prosperity was destroyed by the Depression.

He studied in public schools, then took a degree from the
University of Michigan. His first Broadway play, The Man
Who Had All the Luck (1944), failed, but in 1947, with the
success of All My Sons, his career as one of America's
most distinguished dramatists was launched. His work has
become a standard part of serious dramatic scholarship.
For a bibliographical guide, see Martha T. Eissenstat's
"Arthur Miller: A Bibliography," Modern Drama, V (1962),
93-106. Robert Hogan's book Arthur Miller, 1964, is a
good introduction to his plays. For more detailed studies,
see: Sheila Huftel's Arthur Miller: The Burning Glass,
1965, and Leonard Moss's Arthur Miller, 1967. Dennis
Welland's Arthur Miller, 1961, is a British critic's view.
For scholarly articles about All My Sons, see Arthur Boggs'
"Oedipus and All My Sons," Personalist, XXXXII (1961),
555-560; Richard Loughlin's "Tradition and Tragedy in All
My Sons," English Review, XIV (1964), pp. 23-27; Arvin
Wells's "The Living and the Dead in All My Sons," Modern
Drama, VII (1964), 46-51; Samuel Yorks' "Joe Keller and
His Sons," Western Humanities Review, XIII (Autumn, 1959),
401-407.

The Theatre Season of

1947-1948

The Pulitzer Prize Committee and the Drama Critics
agreed that Tennessee William's powerful Streetcar Named
Desire was the best play of the year. This season also saw
the appearance of a new theatre prize--The Antoinette Perry
Awards, popularly known as the Tony Awards. These
awards, which began under the auspices of the American
Theatre Wing, were named in honor of Antoinette Perry
(1888-1946), a successful director and guiding spirit of the
group. Robert Brustein has stigmatized the Tony awards as
"the exact theatrical equivalent of the Oscars," and the annual presentation as a "tasteless charade" and a "ponderous
ritual of self-praise whose sole criterion of excellence is
the box office." (New Republic, May 23, 1960, pp. 22-23.)
The Tony awards have, however, been bestowed upon many
fine plays such as Arthur Miller's The Crucible (passed
over by both the Pulitzer Committee and the Drama Critics)
and T. S. Eliot's The Cocktail Party. The first Tony Award
went to Mister Roberts by Thomas Heggen and Joshua Logan.
Also running that season were: Command Decision, The
Heiress and Allegro.

STREETCAR NAMED DESIRE

Characters:

Negro Woman	Tamale Vendor
Eunice Hubbel	Blanche DuBois
Stanley Kowalski	Pablo Gonzales
Stella Kowalski	A Young Collector
Steve Hubbel	Nurse
Harold Mitchell (Mitch)	Doctor
Mexican Woman	

Scene I:

When Blanche DuBois, a faded Southern beauty, ar-

rives in New Orleans to visit her sister Stella, she is horrified to find her living in a squalid apartment with her
brutish husband, Stanley Kowalski. She wants to help Stella
financially, but explains that through a series of misfortunes,
she has lost the family plantation in Mississippi.

Scene II:

Stanley, who instinctively dislikes Blanche, questions
her closely about her financial affairs, suspecting that she
has swindled Stella out of her share of their inheritance.

Scene III:

When some of Stanley's coarse friends arrive for an
evening of poker, Blanche and Mitch, the most sensitive of
the lot, are immediately drawn to each other. When Stanley
loses his temper and beats up Stella, who is pregnant,
Blanche encourages her to move to the upstairs apartment.
To her disgust, Stella rejoins Stanley for a night of wild
lovemaking.

Scene IV:

Blanche tries to persuade Stella to leave Stanley, but
Stella insists that she loves her husband in spite of (or because of) his faults. Stanley arrives in time to hear Blanche
describing him as sub-humanoid.

Scene V:

Blanche, disturbed when Stanley says he met a man
who knew her in Mississippi, confides to Stella that she has
been the target of unkind gossips. She also confesses her
hopes that Mitch will marry her.

Scene VI:

That evening, Blanche tells Mitch of her tragic marriage at sixteen to a handsome boy who, she later discovered, was a homosexual and who shot himself when she
revealed her disgust. The sympathetic Mitch embraces
Blanche and declares that they need each other.

Scene VII:

As Stella is preparing for Blanche's birthday party,

Stanley arrives and tells her that he has heard that Blanche lost her teaching job and was virtually run out of Mississippi because of her involvement with a seventeen-year-old boy.

Scene VIII:

Mitch does not come to the party because Stanley has told him Blanche's history. As the dismal celebration proceeds, Blanche suspects that something is amiss and when Stanley makes her a present of a ticket to Mississippi, she collapses.

Scene IX:

That evening after Stanley takes Stella to the hospital to have her baby, Mitch arrives. Complaining that he has never seen Blanche in the light, he thrusts a naked light bulb in her face, examines her faded features, and berates her furiously for lying to him about her age and her past. Blanche explains that grief over her husband's death drove her to promiscuity, but Mitch will have nothing further to do with her.

Scene X:

Blanche, deranged by the scene with Mitch, dresses up in some tawdry finery, and when Stanley returns from the hospital, tells him that she is departing on a cruise with an old admirer. Stanley jeers, then brutally rapes her.

Scene XI:

When Stella comes home from the hospital with her baby and hears Blanche's story about Stanley, she refuses to believe it and decides to have Blanche committed to an asylum. A doctor and nurse arrive, and Blanche, after trying wildly to escape, submits, telling the doctor that she has always had to depend on the kindness of strangers. Stella, uncertain that she has done the right thing, weeps piteously as Blanche is led away; Stanley, abandoning the poker game in the kitchen, tries to comfort her.

Theatre History and Popular Response:

Streetcar Named Desire opened at the Ethel Barrymore Theatre on December 3, 1947 to the plaudits of press

and public. It subsequently ran for 855 performances and
firmly established Tennessee Williams as a playwright of the
first magnitude. The critics called Streetcar "poetic," "a
poignant and luminous story" and a work of "rare discern-
ment and craftsmanship." For representative reviews, see
Commonweal, December 19, 1947, p. 254; Forum, February,
1948, pp. 86-88; Nation, December 20, 1947, p. 686; New
Republic, December 22, 1947, pp. 34-35.

Critical Reputation:

        For a brief introduction to Tennessee Williams' life
and work, see the entry for 1944-1945. The full-length
critical studies of his art cited there contain analyses of
Streetcar Named Desire. For other useful discussions see:
Leonard Berkman's "The Tragic Downfall of Blanche DuBois,"
Modern Drama, X (1967), 249-257; Kenneth Bernard's "The
Mercantile Mr. Kowalski," Discourse, VII (Spring, 1964),
337-340; Constance Drake's "Blanche DuBois: A Re-evalua-
tion," Theatre Annual, XXIV (1968), 58-69; John Gassner's
"Streetcar Named Desire: A Study in Ambiguity," Theatre
in Our Times, 1954, pp. 355-363; Alvin B. Kernan's "Truth
and Dramatic Mode in the Modern Theatre: Chekhov, Piran-
dello, and Williams," Modern Drama, I (1958), 101-114;
Richard Law's "A Streetcar Named Desire as Melodrama,"
Criticism, XIV (1964), 2-8; Joseph Ridell's "A Streetcar
Named Desire--Nietzsche Descending," Modern Drama, V
(1963), 421-430; C. N. Stavron's "Blanche DuBois and Emma
Bovary," Four Quarters, VII (1958), 10-13; and Phillip
Weissman's "Psychological Characters in Current Drama,"
American Imago, XVII (1960), 271-278. For a collection of
essays, see John D. Hurrell, ed., Two Modern American
Tragedies: Reviews and Criticism of 'Death of a Salesman'
and 'Streetcar Named Desire', 1961.

MISTER ROBERTS

Characters:

Chief Johnson	Schlemmer
Lt. (JG) Roberts	Heber
Doc	Dolan
Dowdy	Gerhart
The Captain	Payne
Insigna	Lt. Ann Girard

Mannion   Shore Patrolman, Mil-
Lindstrom   itary Policeman,
Stefanowski   Shore Patrol Officer,
Wiley   Seamen, Firemen,
                           etc.

Act I:

As the war in the Pacific draws to a close, the frustration of Lt. (J.G.) Doug Roberts, increases daily. Young,
idealistic, and eager to get into combat, he finds himself
stuck on a supply ship under the command of a tyrannical
captain who tears up his weekly requests for transfer. The
captain needs Roberts, an exceedingly capable officer, to en-
hance his own record of performance, but he resents the
fact that Roberts takes the part of the men and is rather
contemptuous of his authority. When Mr. Roberts gets the
captain to agree to give the men a leave (they have not had
one for over a year), the Captain extracts Roberts' promise
that he will not send any more letters requesting a transfer
or speak disrespectfully to him.

Act II:

The men go ashore and behave so badly that the ship
is restricted for the rest of its stay. The captain, who
views the incident as a blot on his record, vows the men
will never get another leave. Things go badly for Mr.
Roberts when the men, dismayed because Roberts stops requesting transfers and because he seems more amiable toward the captain, conclude that he is trying for a promotion.
They ostracize him until they accidentally find out about
Roberts' agreement with the captain. The men, chagrined
at their behavior, send in a request for transfer in Roberts'
name and forge the captain's signature. Mr. Roberts is
transferred to the war zone where he is killed, ironically,
while drinking coffee in the wardroom of a ship hit by a
Japanese suicide plane. Upon hearing of Roberts' death,
Ensign Pulver, heretofore interested only in himself, takes
Roberts' place as mediator between the Captain and the men.

Theatre History and Popular Response:

Mister Roberts opened at the Alvin Theatre on February
18, 1948 and ran for 1,157 performances. Both critics and
public were beside themselves with delight and the play was

deemed "a brilliant smash hit, " "magnificent" and "ringing theatre. " Only Louis Kronenburger dissented, but admitted that his was a minority opinion. For representative reviews, see: Life, March 1, 1948, pp. 93-96; New Yorker, February 28, 1948, p. 46; Newsweek, March 1, 1948, pp. 65-66; Theatre Arts, April, 1948, pp. 28-29.

Critical Reputation:

        Thomas Heggen (1919-1949), born at Fort Dodge, Iowa, attended the University of Minnesota, received the Bachelor's Degree in 1941. After graduation, he joined the Navy, and served at Guam, Iwo Jima, and Okinawa. After his discharge in 1945, he joined the editorial staff of Reader's Digest. His novel, Mister Roberts, appeared in 1946 and its success attracted the attention of Joshua Logan, who collaborated with him in writing the stage version. At the age of twenty-nine, at the height of his success, Heggen inexplicably drowned in the bathtub. For a sketch of his life, see Kunitz and Haycraft's Twentieth Century Authors, First Supplement, 1955.

        Joshua Logan (1908-   ), was born in Texarkana, Texas, and grew up in rural Louisiana. He attended Culver Academy and then Princeton, but left without taking a degree in order to study under the famous Stanislavsky at the Moscow Art Theatre. He has subsequently been a successful actor, producer, director, writer, and screenwriter. For further information concerning his life and work consult The Biographical Encyclopedia and Who's Who of the American Theatre, 1966. Mister Roberts has not received any serious scholarly attention, but for brief discussions of the play, consult J. M. Brown's Seeing More Things, 1948, pp. 282-288; George Jean Nathan's Theatre Book of the Year, 1947-48, pp. 283-286; and G. Oppenheimer's Passionate Playgoer, 1958, pp. 574-580.

The Theatre Season of

1948-1949

Arthur Miller's play Death of a Salesman took the
Pulitzer Prize, the Critics' Circle Award and the Tony
Award this season. Miller's tragedy towered over its com-
petition--Anne of a Thousand Days, Detective Story, Life
with Mother, and The Silver Whistle--and established the
playwright in the front rank of American dramatists.

DEATH OF A SALESMAN

Characters:

Willie Loman	Uncle Ben
Linda	Howard Wagner
Biff	Jenny
Happy	Stanley
Bernard	Miss Forsythe
The Woman	Letta
Charley	

Act I:

Willie Loman, travelling salesman, is at sixty-three
reduced to borrowing money from a neighbor, Charley, and
pretending to his wife Linda that he earned it. Furthermore,
he suffers from mental confusion, his mind often wandering
back to the time when his ne'er-do-well sons, Biff and Happy, were young. The boys have not turned out well because
Willie's method of building character stressed popularity as
the key to success but overlooked dishonesty and disobedience.
Biff and Happy, distressed by their father's obvious detachment from reality, try to cheer him with a scheme for borrowing money to open a sporting goods business. Willie,
convinced they will make a fortune, goes to bed happy.

Act II:

The next day, Willie asks for a desk job in the home office, but is fired instead. When he meets Biff and Happy for dinner in a restaurant, he discovers that Biff was refused his loan, and, even worse, has stolen a fountain pen. Willie, puzzling over the reason for Biff's pattern of failure, remembers a time in Boston when Biff discovered him in a hotel room with a woman. While Willie's mind wanders, the boys pick up some women and desert him. Linda, enraged at her sons for leaving Willie, orders them out of the house, whereupon Biff turns on Willie, accusing him of having filled his head with grandiose fantasies instead of letting him discover himself. A little later, Willie leaves in his car, headed for a deliberate smash-up so Biff can inherit his insurance money to go into business.

Requiem

At Willie's graveside, Linda laments that though they had just made the last payment on the house, Willie will never come home again. Biff begs Happy to come out west with him, but Happy, infected with Willie's vain dreams, wants to stay in the city and succeed financially. Biff's haunting remark about Willie sums him up: "He had the wrong dreams.... He never knew who he was."

Theatre History and Popular Response:

Death of a Salesman opened at the Mososco Theatre on February 10, 1949, for a run of 742 performances. Critics and the public alike were astonished by the emotional impact; indeed, the playgoers, transfixed by the play's power, often sat stunned in their seats long after the final curtain. The reviewers agreed that Death of a Salesman was "a play to make history." For representative reviews, see: Commonweal, March 4, 1949, pp. 520-521; Forum, April, 1949, pp. 219-221; Nation, March 5, 1949, pp. 283-284; Theatre Arts, October, 1949, pp. 18-21.

Critical Reputation:

For a brief introduction to Arthur Miller's life and work, see the entry for 1946-1947. The full-length critical works dealing with Miller's plays cited there all contain anal-

yses of Death of a Salesman.   In addition, the following articles discuss various aspects of the play: Sister M. Bettina's
"Willy Loman's Brother Ben: Tragic Insight in Death of a
Salesman," Modern Drama, IV (1962), 409-412; Guerin Bli-
quez's "Linda's Role in Death of a Salesman," Modern Drama,
X (1968), 383-386; Gordon Couchman's "Arthur Miller's Tragedy of Babbitt," Educational Theatre Journal, VII (1955),
206-211; George de Schweinitz's "Death of a Salesman: A
Note on Epic and Tragedy," Western Humanities Review, XIV
(1960), 91-96; John Gassner's "Tragic Perspectives: A Se-
quence of Queries," Tulane Drama Review, II (1958), 7-22;
Ed Gross's "Peddler and Pioneer in Death of a Salesman,"
Modern Drama, VII (1965), 405-410; John Hagopian's "Arthur
Miller: The Salesman's Two Cases," Modern Drama, VI
(1963), 117-125; Joseph Hynes's "Attention Must be Paid...,"
College English, XXIII (1962), 574-578; Esther Jackson's
"Death of a Salesman: Tragic Myth in the Modern Theatre,"
College Language Association Journal (Morgan State College),
VII (1963), 63-76; Sighle Kennedy's "Who Killed the Sales-
man?" Catholic World, May 1950, pp. 110-116; Frank
Kernodle's "The Death of the Little Man," Tulane Drama
Review, I (1956), 46-60; Stephen Lawrence's "The Right
Dream in Miller's Death of a Salesman," College English,
XXV (1964), 547-549; Arthur Oberg's "Death of a Salesman
and Arthur Miller's Search for a Style," Criticism, IX (1967),
303-311; Charlotte Otten's "Who Am I? A Re-investigation
of Arthur Miller's Death of a Salesman," Cresset, XXVI
(1963), 11-13; Brian Parker's "Point of View in Arthur Miller's Death of a Salesman," University of Toronto Quarterly,
XXXV (1966), 144-157; Margaret Ranald's "Death of a Salesman: Fifteen Years After," Comment, III (1965), 28-35;
John Rosenfield's "Inhibitions of the Postwar Reaction,"
Southwest Review, XXXVIII (1953), 347-350; and Paul Siegel's
"Willie Loman and King Lear," College English, XVII (1956),
341-345.   For collections of essays, see John D. Hurrell,
ed., Two Modern American Tragedies: Reviews and Criticism
of 'Death of a Salesman' and 'Streetcar Named Desire', 1961;
and Gerald Weales, ed., Arthur Miller: 'Death of a Salesman': Text and Criticism, 1967.

The Theatre Season of

1949-1950

The Pulitzer Prize this season went to South Pacific, the musical comedy based on James A. Michener's Tales of the South Pacific. The play was written by Oscar Hammerstein, II and Joshua Logan; music and lyrics were by Hammerstein and Richard Rodgers. The drama critics chose Carson McCullers' Member of the Wedding. (The Critics' Circle had considered South Pacific a play of the previous season and had cited it as Best Musical of the Year.) The Tony Award this season went to T. S. Eliot's play The Cocktail Party. Also contending for the awards was Come Back, Little Sheba.

SOUTH PACIFIC

Characters:

Ngana	Abner
Jerome	Stewpot
Henry	Luther Billis
Ensign Nellie Forbush	Professor
Emile de Becque	Lt. Joseph Cable,
Bloody Mary	U.S.M.C.
Bloody Mary's Assistant	Capt. George Brackett,
Yeoman Herbert Quale	U.S.N.
Sgt. Kenneth Johnson	Cmdr. William Harbi-
Seabee Richard West	son, U.S.N.
Seabee Morton Wise	Ensign Cora MacRae
Seaman Tom O'Brien	Ensign Sue Yaeger
Radio Operator Bob	Ensign Lisa Minelli
McCaffrey	Ensign Connie Walewska
Marine Cpl. Hamilton	Ensign Pamela Whitmore
Steeves	Ensign Bessie Noonan
Staff Sgt. Thomas Has-	Liat
singer	Marcel
Lt. James Hayes	Lt. Buzz Adams

Lt. Genevieve Marshall   Islanders, Sailors,
Ensign Dinah Murphy   Marines, and Officers
Ensign Janet MacGregor

Act I:

During World War II Ensign Nellie Forbush, from
Little Rock, Arkansas, stationed somewhere in the South
Pacific, meets Emile de Becque, a wealthy and sophisticated
Frenchman whose plantation is situated on the island outpost.
Despite Nellie's fears that differences in their backgrounds
will make them incompatible, they fall in love, but later,
when Nellie learns that he has two children by a Polynesian
woman, now dead, she determines to break with him. Mean-
while, Lt. Joe Cable falls in love with a young native girl,
Liat, the daughter of rapacious old Bloody Mary. Joe, like
Nellie, fearing that the cultural differences would be insurmountable, sadly decides he cannot marry Liat.

Act II:

When Nellie rejects Becque, he volunteers to go with
Lt. Cable on a dangerous mission to a neighboring island.
Although the mission succeeds, giving the American forces
the upper hand for the first time, Joe dies and for a while
Emile's survival looks uncertain. During this time, Nellie,
sick with fear that Emile will be killed, decides he is the
only man for her. When he returns unharmed, they are
joyously reunited.

Theatre History and Popular Response:

South Pacific opened at the Majestic Theatre on April
7, 1949, and ran for 1,925 performances. Most of the critics were overwhelmingly impressed and hailed the play as
one of the finest musicals ever to appear on the American
stage. A few carped that the play was too sentimental, or,
as Time acidly put it, "a shrewd mixture of tear-jerking and
rib-tickling, of sugar and spice and everything twice." The
public seemed not to notice and some theatregoers paid scalp-
er's prices of as much as $60 a seat to see the show. For
representative reviews, see: Life, April 18, 1949, pp. 93-
96; New Republic, April 25, 1949, pp. 27-28; New Yorker,
April 16, 1949, p. 54; Theatre Arts, June, 1949, p. 15.

Critical Reputation:

     Oscar Hammerstein, II (1895-1960) was born in New York City, a member of one of America's most celebrated theatrical dynasties. He began his schooling at Hamilton Institute, then studied at Columbia (B.A., 1916) and finally went on to law school. He practiced for a year before turning to the theatre. His first hit show was Wildflower (1923); since that time he has been responsible for some of America's best loved musicals--Rose Marie (1924), Desert Song (1926), Show Boat (1927), Oklahoma (1943), Carousel (1945), The King and I (1951), and Flower Drum Song (1958), among others. For more biographical information, see Current Biography, 1944.

     For a brief discussion of Joshua Logan's life and work, see the entry for 1947-1948. Both Hammerstein and Logan are mentioned in the standard histories of the American theatre, but South Pacific has not been the subject of much scholarly attention.

THE MEMBER OF THE WEDDING

Characters:

Berenice Sadie Brown	Helen Fletcher
Frankie Addams	Doris
John Henry West	Sis Laura
Jarvis	T. T. Williams
Janice	Honey Camden Brown
Mr. Addams	Barney Mackean
Mrs. West	

Act I:

     The action takes place during the Second World War, but little of the outside world impinges on Frankie Addams, a gangling twelve-year-old girl who spends much of her time in the kitchen with Berenice, the philosophical old Negress who is Frankie's surrogate mother, and John Henry, Frankie's bespectacled seven-year-old cousin. The first real excitement in her life occurs when her brother Jarvis comes home to be married. Frankie, her adolescent loneliness suddenly galvanized by the arrival of Jarvis and Janice, wants desperately to "belong," and decides to become "a member of the wedding" and go with the bride and groom after the ceremony.

Act II:

Berenice tries to warn Frankie that Jarvis and Janice
may want to be alone, but the impetuous Frankie declares
extravagantly that she will shoot herself in the head if they
do not want her. She fantasizes out loud about how she ex-
pects to discover the wide world and all its people on her
travels with the bride and groom.

Act III:

At the moment of departure, Frankie, dressed out-
landishly for the service, tries to get into the car with her
suitcase, but her father drags her out. Humiliated, Frankie
runs away, threatening to kill herself. At four in the morning, she returns and tells Berenice that all her mad schemes
were childish. When Berenice tells her that John Henry has
been stricken with meningitis in her absence, Frankie pro-
nounces the world "a sudden place."

A month later, Frankie's whole world is changing.
John Henry is dead; Frankie and Mr. Addams are moving to
a new house; Berenice is leaving. Frankie, in the midst of
a new and violent crush on a girl her own age, "belongs" at
last and seems unperturbed.

Theatre History and Popular Response:

The Member of the Wedding opened at the Empire
Theatre on January 5, 1950, and ran for 501 performances.
Audiences usually shouted themselves hoarse after the performances, and the critics, while conceding that the play had
little movement or plot, called it "an absorbing study," full
of "insight, grace, and beauty." Brooks Atkinson summed
it up when he said, "It may not be a play, but it is art."
For representative reviews, see: Commonweal, January 27,
1950, pp. 437-438; New Yorker, January 14, 1950, p. 46;
New Republic, January 30, 1950, p. 28; Theatre Arts,
March, 1950, p. 13.

Critical Reputation:

Carson S. McCullers (1917-1967), born in Columbus,
Georgia, began writing at the age of sixteen. After graduating from high school, she went to New York to go to school,

but having lost her tuition on a subway, took part-time jobs
and went to school at night.   In 1940, her novel The Heart is
a Lonely Hunter attracted wide attention.   Her play Member
of the Wedding began as a successful novel, but with the encouragement of Tennessee Williams, who saw at once the
story's dramatic possibilities, she adapted it for the stage.
For bibliographical information, see Stanley Stewart's "Carson
McCullers: 1940-1956: A Selected Checklist," Bulletin of
Bibliography, XXII (1959), 182-185; and Robert S. Phillips'
"Carson McCullers: 1956-1964: A Selected Checklist," Bul-
letin of Bibliography, XXIV (1964), 113-116.   For a full
length study of Mrs. McCullers' life and work, see Oliver
Evans' Carson McCullers, 1965.   A detailed analysis of The
Member of the Wedding can be found in Gerald Weales'
American Drama Since World War II, 1962, p. 174 ff.   See
also Winifred Dusenbury's Theme of Loneliness in Modern
American Drama, 1960, pp. 58-67 and Robert S. Phillips'
"The Gothic Architecture of The Member of the Wedding,"
Renascence, XVI (1964), 59-72.

THE COCKTAIL PARTY

Characters:

  Edward Chamberlayne   Sir Henry Harcourt-Reilly
  Julia (Mrs. Shuttlethwaite)   Lavinia Chamberlayne
  Celia Coplestone   Nurse-Secretary
  Alexander MacColgie Gibbs   Caterer's Man
  Peter Quilpe

Act I:

       Edward Chamberlayne, a London barrister, finds him-
self awkwardly entertaining friends his wife Lavinia had in-
vited before she suddenly left him.   Among the guests are
Celia, Edward's young mistress; Peter Quilpe, a writer in
love with Celia; Julie, a garrulous old busybody, and Alex,
a bachelor.   Also present is a man no one seems to know,
but who has an uncanny gift for getting people to reveal themselves.   After the other guests depart, the stranger listens
while Edward describes his disappointing marriage.   Later,
when Lavinia comes back home, she and Edward engage in
mutual recriminations, revealing the deep dissatisfaction each
has with the other and with life.

Act II:

Edward, on the advice of his friend Alex, consults a
fashionable psychiatrist, Sir Henry Harcourt-Reilly, who
proves to be the unidentified guest at the party. The doctor
calls in Lavinia and then helps the couple to see themselves
for the first time without illusion. Although each has tried
an affair (Lavinia's lover was Peter Quilpe), neither is capable of giving or receiving love. When they decide to go home
together, the Doctor exhorts them to "work out their salvation with diligence."

Sir Henry's next appointment (arranged by Julia) is
with Celia. The girl, depressed by Edward's rejection and
also by her inability to love Peter, tells Sir Henry that she
has a vague sense of sin and emptiness and wishes to atone.
The doctor warns her that the journey to salvation is a difficult one, but she accepts the challenge. Their work accom-
plished, the three "guardians," Alex, Julia, and Sir Henry,
drink a libation to celebrate the quest of the three seekers.

Act III:

Two years later, at another cocktail party given by
Edward and Lavinia, it is apparent that the guardians have
done their work well. Edward and Lavinia have found a
measure of peace and love within the narrow limits of their
mundane lives. Celia's deliberately chosen path has led her
to immense self-sacrifice and finally to martyrdom at the
hands of hostile savages she had gone into the jungle to help.

Theatre History and Popular Review:

The Cocktail Party which had its world premiere at
the Edinburgh Festival in 1949, began its New York run on
January 21, 1950, at Henry Miller's Theatre, and ended it
409 performances later. The reaction of critics was mixed.
Some called the play the "theatre event of the season," an
"authentic masterpiece," "an absorbing, compassionate, in-
spiring story...." Others, however, complained that the
play was too static, too didactic, too verbose and elusive.
For representative reviews, see: American Mercury, May,
1950, pp. 557-558; Christian Science Monitor Magazine, May
27, 1950, p. 6; Nation, January 28, 1950, pp. 94-95; Saturday Review, February 4, 1950, pp. 28-30.

Critical Reputation:

  Thomas Stearns Eliot (1888-1965) was born at St.
Louis, Missouri, and was educated in private schools. He
attended Harvard (B.A. 1909, M.A. 1910), and studied at
the University of Paris and at Oxford. In 1927, after having
lived in England for several years, he became a British subject. Poet, critic, playwright and editor, Eliot was also a
schoolmaster, a bank clerk and, for most of his life, a director of Faber and Faber, a firm of publishers in London.
A considerable force in the literary world, Eliot played a
major role in the revolution of English poetry with his poem
The Waste Land (1922). Eliot's first play, Murder in the
Cathedral (1935) was a significant contribution to verse drama.
The Cocktail Party, also a verse play, marked Eliot's entry
into the commercial theatre. Eliot was awarded the Nobel
Prize in 1948. For further details of his life, consult Current Biography, 1962. Because Eliot's work has become a
staple part of literary scholarship, a bewildering number of
studies dealing with his art are available. For a bibliographical guide consult Donald Gallup's T. S. Eliot: A Bibliography,
1952. Two excellent full-length studies of a general nature
are F. O. Matthiessen's The Achievement of T. S. Eliot,
3rd edition, 1958; and Grover A. Smith's T. S. Eliot's Poetry
and Plays: A Study in Sources and Meaning, 1956. A more
recent one is P. R. Heading's T. S. Eliot, 1964. For studies of the plays, see D. E. Jones' The Plays of T. S. Eliot,
1960; and Carol H. Smith's T. S. Eliot's Dramatic Theory,
1963. The following critical articles discuss various aspects
of The Cocktail Party: William Arrowsmith's "English Verse
Drama II: The Cocktail Party," Hudson Review, III (1950),
411-430; Paul J. Carter's "Who Understands The Cocktail
Party?", Colorado Quarterly, II (1953), 193-205; Robert A.
Colby's "The Three Worlds of The Cocktail Party: The Wit
of T. S. Eliot," University of Toronto Quarterly, XXIV
(1954), 56-69; Leo Hamalian's "Mr. Eliot's Saturday Evening
Service," Accent, X (1950), 195-206; Thomas Hanzo's "Eliot
and Kierkegaard: 'The Meaning of Happening' in The Cocktail
Party," Modern Drama, III (1960), 52-59; John Hardy's "An
Antic Disposition," Sewanee Review, LXV (1957), 50-60;
Robert Heilman's "Alcestis and The Cocktail Party," Com-
parative Literature, V (1953), 105-116; Robert Heywood's
"Everybody's Cocktail Party," Renascence, III (1950), 28-30;
John Lawlor's "The Formal Achievement of The Cocktail
Party," Virginia Quarterly Review, XXX (1954), 431-451;
John J. McLaughlin's "A Daring Metaphysic: The Cocktail
Party," Renascence, III (1950), 15-28; Russell Robbins' "A

Possible Analogue for The Cocktail Party," English Studies,
XXXIV (1953), 165-167; Edward Schwartz's "Eliot's Cocktail
Party and the New Humanism," Philological Quarterly (Iowa
City) XXXII (1953), 58-68; Nathan Scott's "T. S. Eliot's The
Cocktail Party: Of Redemption and Vocation," Religion in
Life, XX (1951), 286-294; Baird Shuman's "Buddhistic Over-
tones in Eliot's The Cocktail Party," Modern Language Notes,
LXXII (1957), 426-427; Ulrich Weisstein's "The Cocktail
Party: An Attempt at Interpretation on Mythological Grounds,"
Western Review, XVI (1952), 232-241; Jack Winter's "'Pru-
frockism' in The Cocktail Party," Modern Language Quarter-
ly, XXII (1961), 135-148; James Wiseman's "Of Loneliness
and Communion," Drama Critique, V (1962), 14-21; and
Sandra Wool's "Weston Revisited," Accent, X (Autumn, 1950),
207-212.

The Theatre Season of

1950-1951

The Pulitzer Prize Committee elected to withhold its award this season; The Drama Critics chose Darkness at Noon, a dramatization of Arthur Koestler's novel by Sidney Kingsley; and the Tony Award went to Tennessee Williams' The Rose Tattoo. Passed over were The Country Girl and The Autumn Garden.

DARKNESS AT NOON

Characters:

Rubashov	Ivanoff
Guard	Bogrov
402	Hrutsch
302	Albert
202	Luigi
Luba	Pablo
Gletkin	Andre
1st Storm Trooper	Barkeeper
Richard	Secretary
Young Girl	President
2nd Storm Trooper	Soldiers, Sailors, Judges and Jurors

Act I:

In 1937, N. S. Rubashov, once a powerful leader of the Russian Revolution, is arrested and imprisoned. His interrogator, a man named Ivanoff who once served under him in the Red Army, tells him he has been accused of joining a deviationist group and plotting to assassinate the Leader. Rubashov admits to Ivanoff that the reign of terror instituted by the Leader is a perversion of the ideals of the revolution, but he refuses to sign a fake confession even though Ivanoff says he would get a light sentence instead of

114

the death penalty. Gletkin, a brutal young officer, wants to torture Rubashov, but Ivanoff, whose position in the party depends on Rubashov's cooperation, reminds him that the Nazis nearly killed him but only succeeded in stiffening his resistance. When Rubashov returns to his cell, he promises his fellow prisoners to die in silence.

Act II:

Five weeks pass and Rubashov still refuses to sign, but is now tormented by the notion that perhaps the Leader's aims are good and only his repressive measures are evil. Rubashov remembers vividly that he himself lived by the credo that "the end justifies the means." He begins to wonder, too, if he has the right to die, if he could not yet serve the Revolution. Several days later, he is called before the sadistic Gletkin who tells him that Ivanoff has been executed for his poor handling of the Rubashov matter and that he himself is in full charge. He tells Rubashov that he is to die either way, but by confessing he could make his death useful to the Party. When Gletkin stumbles onto Rubashov's weak spot, his bad conscience concerning his mistress, Luba, whom he abandoned when she was arrested and executed by the State, he knows that obtaining Rubashov's confession is just a matter of time.

Act III:

A week later, following his confession in a public court, Rubashov, exhausted and welcoming death, goes to his execution. He mourns for his Revolutionary dreams, realizing that the system he gave his life to build is a barbaric one.

Theatre History and Popular Response:

Darkness at Noon, which opened on January 13, 1951, at the Alvin Theatre, ran for 186 performances. The critical consensus was that Kingsley was a superb craftsman and the play effective drama. Many spoke of it as "gripping," "stunning," and "terrifying," a play of "great emotional and intellectual impact." Inevitably, comparisons were drawn between the play and the Koestler novel. While some critics felt that Kingsley had done a splendid job of dramatizing a difficult book, at least one complained that the intellectual distinction of the novel had evaporated, leaving a "compli-

cated melodrama" containing elements of the "glib propaganda
play." For representative reviews, see: Commonweal,
February 2, 1951, p. 425; Nation, January 27, 1951, pp. 92-
93; Saturday Review, February 3, 1951, pp. 22-24; Theatre
Arts, March, 1951, p. 42.

Critical Reputation:

For a brief introduction to Sidney Kingsley's work
and his position in the drama of America, see the entry for
1933-1934. Darkness at Noon has received little serious
critical attention. For brief discussions of the play, see
John Mason Brown's Dramatis Personae, 1963, pp. 328-331;
and John Gassner's Theatre at the Crossroads, 1960, pp.
141-143.

THE ROSE TATTOO

Characters:

Salvatore	Teresa
Vivi	Father De Leo
Bruno	A Doctor
Assunta	Miss York
Rosa Delle Rose	Flora
Serafina Delle Rose	Bessie
Estella Hohengarten	Jack Hunter
The Strega	The Salesman
Guiseppina	Alvaro Mangiacavallo
Peppina	A Man
Violetta	Another Man
Mariella	

Act I:

In a little village along the coast of the Gulf of Mexico, a town populated largely by Sicilians, Serafina Delle
Rose, a woman of great sensuality and passion, grieves in-
consolably for her husband Rosario. Rosario, a smuggler,
was shot at the wheel of the truck he drove, and Serafina,
nearly unhinged by her sorrow, has had his body cremated
against the priest's orders and keeps his ashes in her house.
Even after the passage of three years, she still refuses to
get dressed or pay attention to her dressmaking business.
When she discovers that her daughter Rosa is attracted to a

young sailor, Serafina locks up the girl's clothes and refuses
to let her out of the house, even to take her final exams at
the high school.   When the women in the village tell Serafina
that Rosario was unfaithful to her, she sobs wildly and prays
for the Virgin to send her a sign.

Act II:

Just when Serafina seems her most slovenly and hysterical, Alvaro Mangiacavallo, a truck driver, makes his appearance.   Serafina is immediately drawn to him because he
reminds her of a comic Rosario.   She sympathizes with him,
for, although he is a bachelor, he has pressing family problems and has just lost his job.   Serafina in turn tells Alvaro
about Rosario's sexual prowess and tenderness, and about the
heart he had tattooed on his chest, a sign which mysteriously
appeared on Serafina's breast when she conceived a child.

Act III:

That evening when Alvaro comes to call, he shows
Serafina the rose he has had tattooed on his chest.   When he
proves to the widow that her husband was in fact unfaithful
to her, she takes him into her bed.   Meanwhile, Serafina
has permitted Rosa to go out with Jack, the young sailor,
though only after making him kneel down and swear to respect Rosa's innocence.   When Rosa comes home and discovers Alvaro with her mother, the mortified Serafina drives
her lover away and then tells Rosa to give herself to her
young man.   As the play ends, Serafina and Alvaro are joyously reunited, and Serafina reveals that once more, the
rose tattoo has appeared on her breast.

Theatre History and Popular Response:

The Rose Tattoo opened on February 3, 1951 and ran
for 306 performances.   Nearly all the critics recognized
faults in the play, a weakness in construction and a lack of
unity.   Some, however, thought the play original, imaginative
and tender, "the loveliest idyll written for the stage in some
time."   Others attacked it as offensive and "perilously close
to burlesque."   One reviewer complained that Williams had
merely exploited "a rather simple biological situation."   For
representative reviews, see: New Yorker, February 10,
1951, p. 58; New Republic, February 19, 1951, p. 22;
Saturday Review, March 10, 1951, pp. 22-24; Time, Febru-

ary 12, 1951, pp. 53-54.

Critical Reputation:

    For a brief introduction to Tennessee Williams' life
and art, consult the entry for 1944-1945. The book-length
critical studies listed there contain analyses of The Rose
Tattoo. A useful article, "The Comic Tennessee Williams,"
by Charles Brooks, can be found in The Quarterly Journal
of Speech, XXXXIV (1958), 275-281.

The Theatre Season of

1951-1952

The Pulitzer Prize went this season to Joseph
Kramm's harrowing play The Shrike. Winner of the Critics'
Circle Award was I Am A Camera, a play by John Van Dru-
ten based on Christopher Isherwood's Berlin Stories. The
Tony Award winner was The Fourposter, by the Dutch play-
wright Jan de Hartog. Also rans: Point of No Return, Mrs.
McThing and Jane.

THE SHRIKE

Characters:

Miss Cardell	Sam Tager
Fleming	George O'Brien
Miss Hansen	Joe Major
Dr. Kramer	Don Gregory
Perkins	John Ankoritis
Grossberg	Frank Carlisle
Dr. Barrow	William Schloss
Patient	Dr. Bellman
Ann Downs	Miss Wingate
Jim Downs	Harry Downs
Dr. Schlesinger	Tom Blair

Act I:

When Jim Downs, depressed about his faltering career
as a Broadway director, tries to commit suicide, his es-
tranged wife Ann has him kept at City Hospital for observation. Now feeling better, encouraged by a new job offer,
and anxious to see his girl friend, Charlotte, Jim makes
plans to leave, only to discover that he is legally confined
to a psychiatric ward.

Act II:

    Jim, growing ever more desperate, is infected by the fear which hangs over the ward--fear of being sent to the section for violent patients or, worse, of being committed to the state mental hospital. He seems unable to convince the doctors that he is sane or to prevent Ann, who hopes he will come back to her, from trying to increase his dependence on her.

Act III:

    Jim's brother Harry comes to visit him and advises him to be a model patient, to pretend to love Ann and agree to go back to her, and to renounce Charlotte. Jim takes Harry's advice, but when he is finally released into Ann's custody, he realizes that she has trapped him for the rest of his life.

Theatre History and Popular Response:

    The Shrike opened at the Cort Theatre on January 15, 1952, and ran for 161 performances. Several reviewers complained that the play was melodramatic and the writing too elementary, but all agreed that The Shrike offered the theatre-goer an evening of intense, if disturbing, entertainment. For representative reviews, see: New Republic, February 4, 1952, p. 23; Saturday Review, February 9, 1952, pp. 22-23; Theatre Arts, March, 1952, p. 71; Time, January 28, 1952, p. 43.

Critical Reputation:

    Joseph Kramm (1907-), born in Philadelphia, Pennsylvania, graduated from the University of Pennsylvania in 1928 and immediately began his career in theatre. After six years with Eva LeGallienne's Civic Repertory Theatre, he began directing and teaching acting. So far, Kramm has not repeated his success of 1951-52, although he did have another play, Giants, Sons of Giants, produced in 1962. His work has received little critical attention. For a biographical sketch, consult Current Biography, 1952.

I AM A CAMERA

Characters:

Christopher Isherwood   Natalia Landauer
Fraulein Schneider   Clive Mortimer
Fritz Wendel   Mrs. Watson-Courtneidge
Sally Bowles

Act I:

        In 1930, Christopher Isherwood, a young British
writer living in Germany, finds himself unable to write. He
contents himself instead with observing life, thinking of himself as a "camera with the shutter open." He meets Sally
Bowles, a flamboyant, somewhat promiscuous nightclub sing-
er, whose attempts to shock him he finds amusing. They
become fast friends, and when she confesses that she is
pregnant by a lover who has abandoned her, Chris offers to
marry her. She decides instead to have an abortion. Meanwhile, Chris's friend Fritz falls in love with Natalia Landauer, a rich young Jewess whom Chris tutors in English.

Act II:

        A week later, Clive Mortimer, a rootless American
millionaire with whom Sally and Chris have struck up a rather parasitic friendship, offers to take them around the world
at his expense. Sally, depressed after her abortion, is delighted, but Chris has misgivings. By joining the idle rich,
he says, they will give up their kinship with the rest of the
world.

        Five days later, Fritz tells them that Natalia's father
does not want her to marry him because he is a Gentile.
Actually, Fritz is a Jew, but because of the anti-Semitism
rampant in Germany, he is reluctant to admit it even to the
Landauers. Just then Sally and Chris learn that Clive has
left without them. Agreeing that it was for the best, they
decide to pull themselves together and get back to work.
They quarrel, however, when Chris realizes Sally is still
hoping for a lucky break (in the form of a rich man) instead
of developing her own talent.

Act III:

        Chris' moral passiveness ends when Natalia is stoned

by a gang of young Nazis and he comes to her defense. He
finally decides to go back to England, after Fritz and Natalia's wedding, to develop and record his impressions, and
to try to live by what he has learned. He begs Sally to
come too, but she has a new lover and wants to stay. Sadly, they say good-bye, realizing they love each other, but
aware that they need more to keep them together.

Theatre History and Popular Response:

        I Am a Camera opened at the Empire Theatre on
November 28, 1951, and ran for 262 performances. Some
critics observed that this play, like The Member of the Wedding, was not really a play at all, but an acting piece,
brought to life by the superb performance of Julie Harris,
who also starred in Member of the Wedding. But even
though the play lacked tension and a sense of direction, reviewers conceded that it was "fascinating" and "a moving
experience." For representative reviews, see: New Republic, December 24, 1951, p. 22; New Yorker, December 8,
1951, p. 62; Saturday Review, December 22, 1951, p. 26;
Theatre Arts, February, 1952, pp. 20-22, 30.

Critical Reputation:

        John Van Druten (1901-1956), naturalized an American
citizen in 1944, was born in London and was educated for
the law. One of his early plays, Young Woodley (1924), an
attack on the British Public School system, was banned in
England, but had a successful run in America. Van Druten
gave up the law in 1926 and came to America as a lecturer.
He subsequently wrote several successful plays--The Voice
of the Turtle (1943), I Remember Mama (1944), and Bell,
Book, and Candle (1950). Although his plays were well received, very little has been written about them. For information on Van Druten's life, see Kunitz and Haycraft's
Twentieth Century Authors, 1942. His place in the American theatre is noted in most of the major studies of American drama; see, for example, George J. Nathan's Theatre in
the Fifties, 1953, pp. 45 ff. Specific discussions of I Am a
Camera can be found in John Mason Brown's As They Appear, 1952, pp. 207-212; John Gassner's "I Am a Camera
and the Chekhov Myth," Theatre at the Crossroads, 1960,
pp. 144-157; and Kenneth Tynan's Curtains, 1961, pp. 247-
248.

THE FOURPOSTER

Characters:

> Agnes
> Michael

Act I:

The play, set entirely in a bedroom containing an enormous fourposter, centers about Michael, a writer, and his wife, Agnes. The First Act shows the tremulous young couple on their wedding night and again a year later, on the night when their first child is born.

Act II:

Ten years later, Michael has become prosperous as a writer, but he and Agnes quarrel bitterly. She tells him he has become a pompous ass since he started writing successful "trash." He counters by telling her he has a mistress who takes an interest in his work, and she strikes back by saying she understands perfectly because she, too, has a romantic interest outside the marriage. As the quarrel ends, Agnes agrees to read part of his new manuscript, but not until the next day.

Another seven years pass, and Agnes and Michael are now worried about their seventeen-year old son who stays out late and whom they mistakenly believe keeps a bottle of whiskey in his room. Michael finally decides to punish the boy, but when he comes home, the astonished father is unable to do or say anything because the boy is wearing a top hat.

Act III:

Five years later, Agnes goes through another crisis on the day her daughter is married. After the wedding, she tells Michael that she wants to leave him. She is no longer content to exist in her husband's shadow but wants one last chance to have a life of her own. Michael shrewdly surmises that Agnes' romantic feelings have been aroused by a young poet who has dedicated his verses to her. She is especially vulnerable because her job as a mother is ending. When Michael insists that she is his inspiration and that he could not get along without her, Agnes is satisfied.

Twelve years later, Michael and Agnes move out,
leaving their house and the fourposter bed for a newly married couple. They agree that the bed has brought them much
happiness. Agnes leaves the bride a little pillow with "God
is Love" stitched on it, and Michael leaves the bridegroom
a bottle of champagne to give him courage.

Theatre History and Popular Response:

The Fourposter opened at the Ethel Barrymore Theatre on October 24, 1951, and ran for 632 performances. Most
of the critics, while conceding that the play was rather thin,
thought it a pleasant enough comedy. One, however, complained that it was "a tedious and uneventful chronicle of the uninteresting married life of a fairly tiresome couple...." For
representative reviews, see: Commonweal, November 9, 1951,
p. 118; New Yorker, November 3, 1951, p. 91; Theatre Arts,
December, 1951, p. 3; Time, November 5, 1951, p. 66.

Critical Reputation:

Jan de Hartog (1914-   ), a Dutchman, was born in
Haarlem but fled the country during the Nazi occupation of
Holland. The Fourposter was written before his departure,
during a ten-week stay in a nursing home where, disguised
as an old woman, he hid from the Germans. In addition to
his work as a playwright, de Hartog also has written novels.
His book The Captain (1966) has been compared to the work
of Joseph Conrad and C. S. Forester. A Quaker, he is
active in humanitarian causes. His book The Hospital (1964),
a muckraking account of deplorable conditions in a Houston
charity hospital where de Hartog and his wife were volunteer
workers, caused a public outcry and was instrumental in
bringing about reform. In 1966, he adopted two Korean or-
phans and since then has written a book, The Children (1969),
for adoptive parents. While writer in residence at the University of Houston, he helped stage the production of his play
William and Mary (1963), and in 1966 his musical comedy
I Do! I Do!, based on The Fourposter, was produced. For
further biographical and bibliographical information consult
Current Biography, 1970. For discussions of the play, see
Abe Laufe's Anatomy of a Hit: Long Run Plays on Broadway
from 1900 to the Present Day, 1966, pp. 241-244; and George
Jean Nathan's Theatre in the Fifties, 1953, pp. 170-172.
The play has received little scholarly interest.

The Theatre Season of

1952-1953

This season William Inge's play Picnic won both the Pulitzer and the Circle Award. The Tony Award went to Arthur Miller's play The Crucible. Also running were Camino Real, On Borrowed Time, The Climate of Eden, The Time of the Cuckoo.

PICNIC

Characters:

Helen Potts   Rosemary Sydney
Hal Carter   Alan Seymour
Millie Owens   Irma Kronkite
Bomber   Christine Schoenwalder
Madge Owens   Howard Bevans
Flo Owens

Act I:

When an earthy young drifter, Hal Carter, comes into a stultifying little Kansas town, his vigorous masculinity disturbs the women he meets. Mrs. Potts, who has spent her life caring for her cranky invalid mother, takes a simple delight in his mere presence in the house, but Flo Owens, her next door neighbor, worries about his effect on her daughters, Millie, a bright tomboy, and Madge, a simple beauty. Rosemary Sydney, an aging, man-hungry spinster, also responds to Hal's vitality.

When Madge's beau, Alan, comes to call, he recognizes Hal as his former college roommate. Mrs. Potts persuades the group to invite Hal to a picnic that evening, and despite Hal's rather unvarnished manners, they agree.

<u>Act II</u>:

     Later that afternoon, Howard Bevans, Rosemary's sometime beau, arrives with a bottle of bootleg whiskey which he passes around to Millie, Hal, and Rosemary, who becomes intoxicated. She makes a desperate pass at Hal, which he gently evades. The humiliated Rosemary then launches a vicious attack on Hal. Howard leads her away, and everyone else leaves for the picnic except Madge and Hal who are to follow later. Madge, who has been drawn to Hal since he arrived, allows him to talk her into staying with him instead of joining the others.

<u>Act III</u>:

     When Howard and Rosemary return that night, Rosemary, who has allowed Howard to seduce her, implores him to marry her, pathetically sobbing that she does not want to live and die an old maid. Howard hedges, then promises to stop by the next morning to talk things over. A little later, Hal and Madge return. Madge is torn between exhilaration and shame because she has made love with Hal, and Hal is hating himself for defiling a virgin.

     The next morning Alan arrives and announces that he has set the police on Hal for stealing a car which in fact Alan had lent him. Then Howard arrives, and Rosemary cleverly traps him into marrying her by having her suitcase packed and her friends assembled, ready to throw rice. As Hal prepares to run from the police, he tells Madge he loves her and asks her to come with him to Tulsa. After he leaves, Madge appears with her suitcase, ready to follow him anywhere.

<u>History and Reviews</u>:

     <u>Picnic</u>, which opened at The Music Box Theatre on February 19, 1953, ran for 477 performances. All the critics agreed that it was a good show, directed as it was by Joshua Logan, but several believed that Logan had taken over Inge's idea and made a good show at the expense of a good play. The playwright himself is reported to have walked out of the theatre in a rage when he saw what Logan had made of the script. For representative reviews, see: <u>America</u>, March 7, 1953, p. 632; <u>Nation</u>, March 7, 1953, p. 213; <u>New Republic</u>, March 16, 1953, pp. 22-23; <u>New</u>

Yorker, February 28, 1953, pp. 65-66; Theatre Arts, May
1953, pp. 14-15.

Critical Reputation:

William Inge (1913-   ), born at Independence, Kansas,
was educated in public schools, then studied speech and
drama at the University of Kansas (A.B., 1935). Later, he
took an M.A. at George Peabody Teachers' College and taught
both in high school and in college. Restless as a teacher,
he became a drama critic and wrote plays himself in a des-
ultory way until he saw The Glass Menagerie in Chicago, an
experience which made him commit himself to serious playwriting. His first big success, Come Back, Little Sheba
(1950), was followed by Picnic, Bus Stop (1955), and Dark
at the Top of the Stairs (1957). His more recent plays, A
Loss of Roses (1960), Natural Affection (1963), and Where's
Daddy (1966), have not received the acclaim that accompanied
some of his earlier work.

Inge's plays have received a fair amount of critical
attention. For a book-length study of his work, see R. B.
Shuman's William Inge, 1965. Allan Lewis discusses Inge in
his American Plays and Playwrights, 1965, pp. 143-163; see
also Gerald Weales' treatment in his American Drama Since
World War II, pp. 40-56. Shuman devotes a chapter to Picnic. For another useful study, consult Eric Bentley's "Pathetic Phalluses," The Dramatic Event, 1954, pp. 102-106.

THE CRUCIBLE

Characters:

Betty Parris	Giles Corey
Tituba	Rev. John Hale
Rev. Samuel Parris	Elizabeth Proctor
Abigail Williams	Francis Nurse
Susanna Walcott	Ezekiel Cheever
Mrs. Ann Putnam	John Willard
Thomas Putnam	Judge Hathorne
Mercy Lewis	Deputy Governor Danforth
Mary Warren	Sarah Good
John Proctor	Hopkins
Rebecca Nurse	

<u>Act I:</u>

In 1692, the town of Salem, Massachusetts, is thrown into a panic when several adolescent girls claim they have been bewitched. As the hysteria increases, the minister, Rev. Parris, sends for Rev. Hale of Beverly, an expert in demonology. When Parris' niece Abigail says Tituba, Parris' Barbadian slave, tried to corrupt her by sorcery, the terrified Negress confesses to commerce with the devil, and she and the girls accuse several more women of witchcraft.

<u>Act II:</u>

Four judges from Boston and Deputy Governor Danforth arrive to try the accused, many of whom the villagers know to be of unimpeachable character. One of the accused, Elizabeth Proctor, had recently dismissed Abigail from her household when she discovered that her husband, John, and Abigail were having an affair. When Elizabeth is taken, John seizes Mary Warren, the Proctor's present serving girl, and forces her to admit that she and the other girls are only pretending to be possessed.

<u>Act III:</u>

John drags Mary into court where she confesses the fraud, but Abigail denies it and accuses Mary of witchcraft. Proctor, in a rage, tells the court of his relations with Abigail and explains that she still loves him and wants to get rid of Elizabeth. Proctor's testimony is discredited, however, when Elizabeth, testifying separately, tries to protect her husband by denying he is a lecher. When Proctor himself is accused by the hysterical girls, Rev. Hale quits the courtroom in disgust, denouncing the proceedings.

<u>Act IV:</u>

Proctor, now awaiting execution, is offered his freedom if he will confess and name the other witches. He refuses. The Rev. Hale urges Elizabeth to get Proctor to lie to save himself, but Elizabeth cries out as her husband approaches the gallows: "He have his goodness now. God forbid I take it from him!"

Theatre History and Popular Response:

The Crucible opened at the Martin Beck Theatre on
January 22, 1953, for a run of 197 performances. Although
the play had an undeniable impact, most reviewers found it
less than satisfactory. Several observed, for example, that
Miller failed to delve into the causes and motives which created the story. He had, one said, written a polemic which
appealed to the intellect but not to the heart. Most were
aware that the play was a political parable with certain obvious resemblances to the McCarthy hearings, before which
Miller himself had been called to testify. In Miller's defense, however, few reviewers felt that he had pressed the
parallels too far. For representative reviews, see: Commentary, March 1953, pp. 265-271; Life, February 9, 1953,
pp. 87-88; New Republic, February 16, 1953, pp. 22-23;
Theatre Arts, April 1953, pp. 24-26, 65-69.

Critical Reputation:

For a brief introduction to Miller's life and work,
see the entry for 1946-1947. The book-length studies of his
art cited there contain analyses of The Crucible. For critical articles which discuss the play, see the following: Richard Cassell's "Arthur Miller's 'Rage of Conscience'," Ball
State Teachers' College Forum, I (1960-1961), 31-36; Penel-
ope Curtis' "The Crucible," Critical Review, VIII (1965),
45-58; James Douglas' "Miller's The Crucible: Which Witch
is Which?" Renascence, XV (1963), 145-151; Stephen Fender's
"Precision and Pseudo-Precision in The Crucible," Journal
of American Studies, I (1967), 87-98; Phillip Hill's "The
Crucible: A Structural View," Modern Drama, X (1967),
312-317; Henry Popkin's "Arthur Miller's The Crucible,"
College English, XXVI (1964), 139-146; and Phillip Walker's
"Arthur Miller's The Crucible: Tragedy or Allegory?,"
Western Speech, XX (1956), 222-224.

The Theatre Season of

1953-1954

The most celebrated play this season was The Teahouse of the August Moon, which won the Pulitzer Prize, the
Circle Award, and the Tony Award. The play, John Pat-
rick's adaptation of the Vern Sneider novel, won over Tea
and Sympathy, The Caine Mutiny Court Martial, and Take a
Giant Step.

THE TEAHOUSE OF THE AUGUST MOON

Characters:

Sakini	Mr. Sumata
Sergeant Gregovich	Mr. Sumata's Father
Col. Wainwright Purdy III	Mr. Seiko
Captain Fisby	Miss Higa Jiga
Old Woman	Mr. Keora
Old Woman's Daughter	Mr. Oshira
The Daughter's Children	Villagers
Lady Astor	Ladies' League for
Ancient Man	Democratic Action
Mr. Hokaida	Lotus Blossom
Mr. Omura	Captain McLean

Act I:

When Col. Wainwright Purdy III, an officer in the
American occupation forces on Okinawa following World War
II, sends Captain Fisby to Tobiki, an outlying village, to
teach the natives the democratic process as conceived by the
Army's Plan B, he has no idea what the young American
will be up against. Fisby, accompanied by a shrewd native
interpreter, Sakini, greets the people and receives their
gifts (Okinawans know how to receive conquerers), but when
he suggests a few basic changes in village life--such as having a school and electing officials--they seem to understand

130

very little.   Nor does Fisby understand when they present
him with Lotus Blossom, a geisha girl.

Act II:

At first, Fisby's troubles seem insurmountable.
Lotus Blossom excites the envy of the rest of the village
women, particularly the newly established Ladies' League
for Democratic Action; the villagers show a decided lack of
interest in constructing a school; and the local industry Fisby
proposed falters when no one wants to buy the trinkets they
make for sale.   As Fisby gradually succumbs to the charm
of village life, Plan B seems less and less appropriate or
desirable.   Instead, he allows Lotus to teach the women
geisha lessons, authorizes the natives to build a teahouse instead of a school, and finally, settles on another enterprise
for the Tobikans--the marketing of their sweet potato brandy
(ready in only ten days) to the army of occupation.   Col.
Purdy, suspecting that Fisby has lost his wits, sends a psychiatrist, Captain McLean, to spy on him, but McLean, too,
"goes native."

Act III:

Fisby's scheme succeeds wildly, and the natives, now
enormously successful and happy, give Fisby a party in the
beautiful new teahouse to show their gratitude.   During the
festivities, the horrified Col. Purdy appears and orders the
teahouse and the stills dismantled.   As Fisby sadly bids his
friends farewell, the Colonel rushes in and begs everyone to
help him reassemble everything.   It seems that Fisby's
scheme impressed the brass in Washington; in fact, photographers and junketing congressmen were on the way.   The
wily Tobikans, who have only hidden the stills and materials
for the teahouse, reassemble everything in a matter of minutes, then settle down to celebrate.

Theatre History and Popular Reviews:

When Teahouse opened at the Martin Beck Theatre
on October 15, 1953, it was enthusiastically proclaimed, ran
for 1,027 performances, and went on to international fame
when it toured Europe and the Orient.   The play, hailed as
the most enchanting comedy in many a season, had a delicate
blend of satire, masterful characterization, and a great deal
of wisdom underlying the fun.   For representative reviews,

see: Nation, October 31, 1953, pp. 357-358; New Republic,
October 26, 1953, p. 21; Saturday Review, October 31, 1953,
p. 29; Theatre Arts, December, 1953, pp. 22-24.

Critical Reputation:

        John Patrick (1905-   ), born at Louisville, Kentucky,
and educated at Columbia and Harvard, began his career as
a dramatist by writing radio plays for Helen Hayes.   His
first Broadway play, Hell Freezes Over (1935), was followed
by The Willow and I (1942), a critical success but not a popular one.   His experiences in World War II provided him the
inspiration for his next play, The Hasty Heart (1945).   The
year 1950 saw the production of two light comedies, Curious
Savage and Lo and Behold; neither, however, was well received.   So far, his major achievement is Teahouse, an
enormous commercial success, but one which has received
little critical attention.   For a biographical sketch of the
author, see Biographical Encyclopedia and Who's Who of the
American Theatre, 1966.

The Theatre Season of

1954-1955

The Pulitzer Prize Committee and the Drama Critics gave the Best Play Award this season to Tennessee Williams' blistering play, Cat on a Hot Tin Roof. The Tony Award went to Joseph Hayes' crime drama, The Desperate Hours. Also in the running were The Flowering Peach, The Bad Seed, Bus Stop, and Inherit the Wind.

CAT ON A HOT TIN ROOF

Characters:

Lacey	Sonny
Sookey	Trixie
Margaret	Big Daddy
Brick	Reverend Tooker
Mae	Doctor Baugh
Gooper	Daisy
Big Mama	Brightie
Dixie	Small
Buster	

Act I:

When Margaret--Maggie the Cat--learns that her father-in-law, Big Daddy, has cancer, she fears that her husband's rapacious brother, Gooper, and his social climbing wife, Mae, will wrest Big Daddy's huge Mississippi Delta plantation away from her alcoholic husband, Brick. Even though Big Daddy has always favored Brick, his drinking and her childlessness (Gooper and Mae expect their sixth) seriously weaken his position. Maggie, who grew up dependent on patronizing relatives, wants her share, but Brick has little interest in anything but his emotional problems, which are considerable, the result of a homosexual attachment to his friend Skipper, who subsequently committed suicide.

Brick's emotional disturbance manifests itself not only in
his dependence on the bottle, but in his refusal to sleep
with Maggie, causing her enormous anguish and preventing
her from having a child which could secure their position
with Big Daddy.

Act II:

After a family celebration of Big Daddy's birthday,
a rather strained occasion since everyone except Big Mama
and Big Daddy knows it will be his last, Big Daddy con-
fronts Brick about his drinking. Brick tells his father that
he needs liquor to escape the lying and hypocrisy he finds
all around him. Big Daddy, too, confesses that his whole
life has been a lie and that most of his relationships are
essentially false. Then Big Daddy bluntly tells his son that
Brick lies to himself about Skipper when he insists that
theirs was only pure friendship. Stunned, Brick retaliates
by telling Big Daddy he is dying.

Act III:

After Big Mama is told the truth about Big Daddy's
illness, Gooper shows his hand by announcing that he has
drawn up a trusteeship of the property. Big Mama, who
recognizes that Gooper plans to cut Brick out, pleads with
him and Maggie to have a child before Big Daddy dies.
Maggie boldly states that she is already pregnant, and Brick
does not deny it. Later, the indomitable Maggie locks up
Brick's liquor and tells him that he can have it back only
after he makes the lie come true.

Theatre History and Popular Reviews:

When this stunning play opened at the Morosco Theatre on March 24, 1955, for a run of 694 performances, the
critical consensus was that Cat on a Hot Tin Roof was a
powerful and significant drama. A few complained about the
explicitness of the language and the homosexual theme, but
the play has gone down as a landmark in the literature of
the American theatre. For representative reviews, see:
Nation, April 9, 1955, pp. 314-315; New Republic, April 11,
1955, pp. 28-29; New Yorker, April 2, 1955, p. 68; Time,
April 4, 1955, p. 98; Theatre Arts, June, 1955, 18-19, 22-
23.

Critical Reputation:

For an introduction to Tennessee Williams' life and
works, see the entry for 1944-1945. For specific discussions of Cat on a Hot Tin Roof, the following articles are
useful: William Becker's "Reflections on Three New Plays, "
Hudson Review, VIII (Summer, 1955), 268-272; Bernard Dukore's "The Cat Has Nine Lives, " Tulane Drama Review,
VIII (1963), 95-100; William Sacksteder's "The Three Cats:
A Study in Dramatic Structure, " Drama Survey, V (1966),
252-266; Vernon Young's "Social Drama and Big Daddy, "
Southwest Review, XLI (1956), pp. 194-197. The book length
studies cited at 1944-1945 which treat Williams' life and art
also contain analyses of the play.

THE DESPERATE HOURS

Characters:

Tom Winston	Glenn Griffin
Jesse Bard	Hank Griffin
Harry Carson	Robish
Eleanor Hilliard	Chuck Wright
Ralphie Hilliard	Mr. Patterson
Dan Hilliard	Lt. Carl Fredericks
Cindy Hilliard	Miss Swift

Act I:

When Jesse Bard, Deputy Sheriff of Indianapolis,
learns that Glenn Griffin, Glenn's brother Hank, and one
other convict have escaped from the federal penitentiary 70
miles away, he knows they will head for Indianapolis to pick
up Glenn's girlfriend and to settle the score with Bard, who
had apprehended Griffin and broken his jaw. The convicts
arrive and force their way into the suburban home of Dan
Hilliard. They hold his terrified wife Eleanor at gun point,
and when the rest of the family returns that evening, Griffin
makes it plain that he will kill any or all of them if they resist or signal for help. The anxious family and the vicious
trio settle down to wait for midnight when Glenn's girl is due
to arrive with some money.

Act II:

Because Glenn's girl was unavoidably detained, she has

mailed the money, which means the convicts will stay at the
Hilliards somewhat longer than planned. They force Dan
and Cindy to go to work as usual, but insist that Ralphie,
Dan's impetuous son who has already tried unsuccessfully to
run for help, stay home from school. During the day, the
police discover Glenn's hiding place, but are reluctant to
smoke him out for fear the Hilliards will be harmed.

Act III:

The police take up a position in an attic next door.
They finally decide to try to apprehend the convicts, but
Dan, frantic about the safety of his family, pleads for ten
minutes before they go in. Dan goes home with an unloaded
gun, forces a showdown with Glenn, who takes Dan's gun
and grabs Ralphie to use as a hostage. Ralphie runs to
safety after Dan tells him the gun is not loaded. Dan then
has Glenn at bay, but cannot bring himself to shoot him.
Glenn runs outside and is shot by Bard. The Hilliards,
conscious of their miracle, are happily reunited.

Theatre History and Popular Response:

The Desperate Hours opened at the Ethel Barrymore
Theatre on February 10, 1955, and ran for 212 performances.
Most reviewers agreed that the play was momentarily gripping, but several commented that Hayes had sacrificed psychological implications for action and made no attempt to ex-
plore the criminal mind. For representative reviews, see:
Nation, February 26, 1955, p. 186; New Yorker, February
19, 1955, pp. 76-77; Saturday Review, February 26, 1955,
p. 22; Time, February 21, 1955, p. 54.

Critical Reputation:

Joseph Hayes (1918-), was born at Indianapolis, Indiana,
and was educated at Indiana University (B.A. 1941). Hayes, a
full-time professional playwright, has written, in collaboration
with his wife, a number of plays for amateur production. In addition, he is also a novelist and occasional producer of Broadway plays. For further information on his life and work, see
Biographical Encyclopedia and Who's Who of the American Theatre, 1966. For an analysis of The Desperate Hours, which has
otherwise received little attention, see The Dramatic Experience
by Judah Bierman, James Hart, and Stanley Johnson, 1958, pp.
16-22. On pages 72-78 of the same book, Joseph Hayes discusses the construction of his play.

The Theatre Season of

1955-1956

This season the Pulitzer Prize, the Circle Award,
and the Tony Award all went to The Diary of Anne Frank, a
moving play based on The Diary of a Young Girl, the "un-
bosomings" of a Jewish girl growing up while in hiding from
the Nazis. Masterfully adapted by Frances Goodrich and Albert Hackett, the play defeated A View From the Bridge, The
Ponder Heart, No Time for Sergeants, A Hatful of Rain, and
Middle of the Night. This season also marked the beginning
of a new annual prize for drama--The Village Voice Off-
Broadway Award--known as the Obie. The first Obie was
awarded to the play Absolom, by the British critic Lionel
Abel.

THE DIARY OF ANNE FRANK

Characters:

Mr. Frank	Mrs. Frank
Miep	Margot Frank
Mrs. Van Daan	Anne Frank
Mr. Van Daan	Mrs. Kraler
Peter Van Daan	Mr. Dussel

Act I:

Following the liberation of Europe in 1945, Otto Frank
makes a sad pilgrimage to the attic hideout in Amsterdam
where he lived with his family during the Nazi occupation of
Holland. Here he finds the diary his sprightly daughter Anne
kept during the three years they spent in the "secret annex,"
years in which Anne changed from a mischievous child to a
spirited young woman of 16. The main part of the play con-
sists of dramatizations of passages from the journal.

When the Franks, together with the Van Daan family,
go into hiding above a warehouse, they must maintain strict

137

silence during the day, a problem which hits the lively Anne
hardest.   To make matters worse, they are joined by a fussy dentist, Mr. Dussel, who becomes Anne's roommate and
who insists on strict order.   Things improve at night, however, for after the building empties, the refugees can move
about normally.   One night a thief breaks into the building,
and the Jews realize that at least one person knows of their
hiding place.

Act II:

        The months drag by, becoming years.   The misery of
the families increases as the food supply becomes shorter.
For Anne, at least, life is bearable because she and young
Peter Van Daan have become fast and loving friends.   Everyone's hopes are raised when news of the Allied invasion
reaches them, but these hopes are shattered when Mr. Kra-
ler, the owner of the warehouse and their protector, reveals
that he is being blackmailed by one of his workers who suspects he is hiding Jews.   Suddenly one day the thing they
have all feared happens: the Green Police come, break down
the door, and drag the Jews away.

        The play ends as Mr. Frank, the only member of the
group to survive the concentration camps, finds this state-
ment in Anne's diary: "In spite of everything, I still believe
that people are really good at heart.   Sadly, Mr. Frank confesses that Anne puts him to shame.

Theatre History and Popular Response:

        The Diary of Anne Frank opened on October 5, 1955,
at the Cort Theatre and ran for 717 performances.   Later,
it played all around the world.   In Germany it became something of a national penance; people flocked to see it and after
the final curtain sat frozen in their seats, sledgehammered
by the impact of the play.   The reviewers agreed that the
play's success arose from its absence of theatrical tricks,
attempts at tear-jerking, or melodrama.   What could have
so easily degenerated into a maudlin piece of social comment
was crafted by the Hacketts into a monument to an unquench-
able human spirit.   For representative reviews, see: Commentary, November, 1955, pp. 464-467; Nation, October 29,
1955, p. 370; Newsweek, October 17, 1955, p. 103; Saturday
Review, October 22, 1955, p. 27.

Critical Reputation:

      Albert Hackett and Frances Goodrich (who is Mrs.
Hackett) began collaborating in 1930 with the stage play Up
Pops the Devil.   Since that time, they have written and
adapted literally dozens of screen plays--The Thin Man, Father of the Bride and Lady in the Dark, to mention only a
few.   Frances Goodrich was born at Belleville, New Jersey,
and studied theatre at Vassar.   She later studied at the New
York School of Social Service but abandoned social work to
become an actress.   Albert Hackett, born in New York City
in 1900, a child actor by the time he was six, came from a
theatrical family and attended Professional Children's School.
For a biographical account, see Current Biography, October,
1956, pp. 216-218.   Neither the Hacketts nor their play
Diary of Anne Frank has been the subject of scholarly investigation.

The Theatre Season of

1956-1957

The Pulitzer Prize, the Circle Award, and the Tony
Award all went this season to Eugene O'Neill's memorable
Long Day's Journey Into Night, the play he had hoped to sup-
press until twenty-five years after his death. Also running
were: Orpheus Descending, A Moon for the Misbegotten, A
Clearing in the Woods, and Auntie Mame.

LONG DAY'S JOURNEY INTO NIGHT

Characters:

James Tyrone	Edmund Tyrone
Mary Cavan Tyrone	Cathleen
James Tyrone, Jr.	

Act I:

During the course of a long summer day in 1912,
James Tyrone, an actor, and his tormented family make
some terrifying discoveries about themselves. As the day
begins, Tyrone's pretty, nervous little wife Mary begins to
show signs that her most recent "cure" for morphine addiction has failed to work. According to Jamie, Tyrone's older
son and a wastrel, Mary's addiction is the result of Tyrone's
stinginess, for at the time of Edmund's birth Tyrone summoned a cut-rate inferior doctor whose prescription caused
her dependence on the drug.

Act II:

By lunchtime, Mary is so remote that the three men
know she has taken a large dose of the medicine. She complains absently that she has no friends, that Tyrone never
wanted a house but preferred hotels and the company of men
in barrooms. As her detachment increases she recalls her
happy girlhood, her years in a convent school, and the early

140

days of her marriage to Tyrone, who was then a stage idol.
Meanwhile, Edmund, the younger son, suspected of having
consumption, leaves for the doctor's office, begging his
mother to have the faith and the will to control her habit.
Alone, Mary cries piteously to the Virgin to help her.

Act III:

When Edmund and Tyrone return, Edmund tries to
tell his mother that he has tuberculosis but Mary is so far
gone on drugs that she cannot comprehend the truth.   The
frustrated Edmund calls her a dope fiend, then, conscience-
stricken, leaves the house.   Mary, shattered by Edmund's
outburst, departs for her room in spite of James' pleas that
she not take any more poison.

Act IV:

Late at night, when Edmund comes in, he and his
father, both thoroughly drunk, play cards and talk.   Alternately, they argue and then exchange confidences.   Edmund accuses his father of trying to economize by putting
him into an inferior sanitorium.   Tyrone talks about his
impoverished childhood, then sadly reveals that he threw
away a promising career as a Shakespearean actor in order
to play popular roles which paid more.   Edmund, something
of a mystic, tries to describe several experiences he had
when he felt he had transcended himself.   Later, when Jamie
comes home from a whorehouse, gloriously drunk, he confesses to Edmund his deep-seated jealousy, but also says
that Edmund is the only person he really loves.

Suddenly Mary appears, dragging her faded wedding
gown.   Oblivious to everyone in the room she talks wildly
of the past when she married James Tyrone and "was so
happy for a time."   The three men sit staring at each other
as the curtain falls.

Theatre History and Popular Response:

Long Day's Journey Into Night had its first public
production in Stockholm in 1956, some three years after
O'Neill's death.   The American production opened at the
Helen Hayes Theatre on November 7, 1956, and ran for
390 performances.   Some critics alluded in passing to the
play's prolixity and to its structural faults, but all conceded

it was a stunning achievement. "A magnificent and shattering play, " wrote one. Said another, "It restores the drama
to literature and the theatre to art. " For representative reviews, see: Commonweal, February 1, 1957, pp. 467-468;
Saturday Review, November 24, 1956, pp. 30-31; Theatre
Arts, January, 1957, pp. 25-26; Time, November 19, 1956,
p. 57.

Critical Reputation:

       A brief introduction to Eugene O'Neill's life and work
can be found at the entry for 1919-1920. The full length
studies of his art cited there contain analyses of Long Day's
Journey Into Night. Robert Brustein's Theatre of Revolt,
1962, contains a useful discussion of the play (pp. 348-358).
See also the following scholarly articles: Edwin A. Engel's
"Eugene O'Neill's Long Day's Journey Into Light, " Michigan
Alumni Quarterly Review, LXIII (1957), 348-354; Sidney
Finkelstein's "O'Neill's Long Day's Journey, " Mainstream,
XVI (1963), 47-51; Robert Lee's "Eugene O'Neill's Remem-
brance: The Past is the Present, " Arizona Quarterly, XXIII
(1967), 293-305; Jordan Y. Miller's "Eugene O'Neill's Long
Day's Journey, " The Kansas Magazine, 1958, pp. 77-81;
John H. Raleigh's "O'Neill's Long Day's Journey Into Night
and New England Irish-Catholicism, " Partisan Review, XXVI
(Fall, 1959), 573-592; Grant Redford's "Dramatic Art vs.
Autobiography: A Look at Long Day's Journey Into Night, "
College English, XXV (1964), 527-535; Annette Rubenstein's
"The Dark Journey of Eugene O'Neill, " Mainstream, X
(April, 1957), 29-33; John T. Shawcross's "The Road to
Ruin: The Beginning of O'Neill's Long Day's Journey, "
Modern Drama, III (1960), 289-296; Phillip Weissman's
"Conscious and Unconscious Autobiographical Dramas of
Eugene O'Neill, " Journal of the American Psychoanalytic
Association, V (1957), 432-460; and Sophus Keith Winther's
"O'Neill's Tragic Themes: Long Day's Journey Into Night, "
Arizona Quarterly, XIII (1957), 295-307.

The Theatre Season of

1957-1958

The winner of both the Pulitzer Prize and the Circle
Award this season was Look Homeward, Angel, Ketti Frings'
adaptation of Thomas Wolfe's mountainous novel. Sunrise at
Campobello by Dore Schary won the Tony award over The
Dark at the Top of the Stairs, Two for the Seesaw, West
Side Story, The Rope Dancers, and The Music Man. End-
game by the Irish-French playwright Samuel Beckett, won the
Obie Award.

LOOK HOMEWARD, ANGEL

Characters:

Ben Gant	Mrs. Snowden
Mrs. Marie "Fatty" Pert	Mr. Farrell
Helen Gant Barton	Miss Brown
Hugh Barton	Laura James
Eliza Gant	W. O. Gant
Will Pentland	Dr. McGuire
Eugene Gant	Tarkington
Jake Clatt	Madame Elizabeth
Mrs. Clatt	Luke Gant
Florry Mangle	

Act I:

In 1916 in Altamont, North Carolina, Eliza Gant, an
aggressive and acquisitive woman, bullies her family, dab-
bles in real estate, and runs the Dixieland, a shabby boarding
house. Rebellion in the family, however, is a constant threat.
Her husband, a stonecutter, occasionally stages titanic drunks
which mortify Eliza before her seedy boarders, and Ben, one
of her older sons, is having an affair with a woman in her
forties. Eugene, a restless, seventeen-year-old dreamer,
resents his enslavement by Eliza and longs to go away to col-

143

lege, but the miserly Eliza, insisting she cannot afford the
expense, refuses to send him. When a 23-year-old woman,
Laura James, comes to stay at the Dixieland, she and Gene
are immediately drawn to each other.

Act II:

Eliza, no sentimentalist where a profit can be turned,
tries to get her husband to sell his marble yard and the
large Carrara angel which reminds him of his lost youth and
dreams. He finally agrees to the sale but announces that he
plans to use the money to go away with Eugene and put him
in school. Outsmarted, Eliza backs down. A little later,
Ben, who suffers from tuberculosis, collapses and dies.

Act III:

Two weeks later, Eliza tries to prevent Gene's marriage to Laura (who has already declined the offer), by of-
fering to send him to school. When mother and son part,
the love they bear for each other in spite of their conflicts
breaks through for a moment, but Eliza relapses and sends
him off with a volley of platitudes.

Theatre History and Popular Response:

Look Homeward, Angel, which opened at the Ethel
Barrymore Theatre on November 20, 1957, was warmly re-
ceived by critics and subsequently ran for 564 performances.
Miss Frings was lavishly praised for doing what seemed an
impossible job--"the herculean task of jamming this steamer
trunk of a book into the tight confines of the stage...," as
John Toohey expressed it (A History of the Pulitzer Prize
Plays, p. 296). For representative reviews, see: America,
February 8, 1958, p. 551; New Yorker, December 7, 1957,
pp. 93-95; Theatre Arts, February, 1958, pp. 18-19; Time,
December 9, 1957, p. 72.

Critical Reputation:

Ketti Frings was born in Columbus, Ohio, and studied
at Principia College. She began her career by writing advertising copy and went on to work as a columnist, radio
script writer, and movie magazine ghost writer. Although
her name was not generally familiar to audiences before

Look Homeward, Angel, her work as a screenwriter has
made her well known in Hollywood circles. She wrote Hold
Back the Dawn in 1942 and the screen versions of Come Back
Little Sheba (1952) and The Shrike (1955). For further de-
tails, see Current Biography, 1960, pp. 151-153. Miss
Frings' adaptation of Look Homeward, Angel has received lit-
tle scholarly attention. For a note on the play, see John
Gassner's Theatre at the Crossroads, 1960, pp. 294-296.
See also Abe Laufe's Anatomy of a Hit, 1966, pp. 313-318.

SUNRISE AT CAMPOBELLO

Characters:

Anna Roosevelt	Miss Marguerite (Missy)
Eleanor Roosevelt	LeHand
Franklin D. Roosevelt, Jr.	Doctor Bennet
James Roosevelt	Franklin Calder
Elliott Roosevelt	Stretcher Bearers
Edward	Mr. Brinner
Franklin D. Roosevelt	Mr. Lassiter
John Roosevelt	Gov. Alfred E. Smith
Marie	Daly
Louis McHenry Howe	Policeman
Mrs. Sara Delano Roosevelt	Sen. Walsh
	A Speaker

Act I:

     While vacationing with his family at their summer
home in New Brunswick, Canada, Franklin Delano Roosevelt,
then about forty, is stricken with infantile paralysis. Although his health is the immediate concern, the outlines of
the impending conflict are clear. Will he retire to his home
at Hyde Park and live out his days as a country squire, as
his dominating mother insists he should, or will he continue
his political career, as his wife Eleanor and his long-time
political friend Louis Howe hope he will?

Act II:

     A year or so later, Franklin, though occasionally ir-
ritable and discouraged, is making his adjustment to paralysis. Eleanor, once rather retiring, has taken to making
speeches and working in the party in order to keep her husband's name alive until he recovers sufficiently to re-enter

public life himself.

Act III:

  Franklin is asked to head Al Smith's campaign for
the Democratic Presidential nomination. In the play's cli-
mactic moment, Franklin, amid wild cheering by the con-
vention delegates, walks the ten agonizing steps to the podium
to place Smith's name in nomination.

Theatre History and Popular Response:

  Sunrise at Campobello opened on January 30, 1958,
at the Cort Theatre and ran for 556 performances. Most of
the reviewers praised the play, calling it "tremendously
moving, " "a stirring and heroic portrait, " a play that "proceeds from one theatrically golden achievement to another."
A dissenting voice declared that the play lacked subtlety and
presented paper cut-outs for characters. For representative
reviews, see: Christian Century, May 21, 1958, p. 622-
623; Life, February 10, 1958, pp. 91-94; New Yorker, February 8, 1958, pp. 93-96; Time, February 10, 1958, p. 57.

Critical Reputation:

  Dore Schary (1905-) was born in Newark, New Jersey, the child of immigrants from Central Europe. He attended public high school but left without graduating. After
holding various jobs, he returned to school and completed
the four-year course in ten months. He worked for a time
on a newspaper, then went on to become a successful screen
writer, director and producer. Although Schary is known
primarily for his work in motion pictures, Sunrise at Campobello was the first of several plays he wrote for the theatre.
For further information concerning his life and work, consult Biographical Encyclopedia and Who's Who of the American Theatre, 1966. For a brief discussion of Schary's plays,
including Sunrise at Campobello, see Allan Lewis' American
Plays and Playwrights, 1965, pp. 161-162. Otherwise, the
play has not been the subject of much scholarly interest.

The Theatre Season of

1958-1959

This season Archibald MacLeish's verse drama J. B. took both the Pulitzer Prize and the Tony Award. The Circle Award went to Raisin in the Sun by Lorraine Hansberry. A foreign play, The Quare Fellow, by the Irish playwright Brendan Behan, won the Obie. Also running during this exciting season were A Touch of the Poet, Sweet Bird of Youth, The Disenchanted, and The Pleasure of His Company.

J. B.

Characters:

First Roustabout	Rebecca
Second Roustabout	The Girl
Nickles	Mrs. Botticelli
Mr. Zuss	Mrs. Lesure
Prompter	Mrs. Adams
J. B.	Mrs. Murphy
Sarah	Jolly
David	Bildad
Mary	Zophar
Jonathan	Eliphaz
Ruth	

Prologue:

In the corner of a tent, part of a traveling circus "which has been on the roads of the world for a long time," a balloon man, Mr. Zuss, and a popcorn vender, Nickles, discuss the significance of the story of J. B., a modern Job, which is about to be performed. Mr. Zuss dons a God mask and Nickles a Satan mask, and together, as in the old moralities, they vie for the soul of J. B.

147

Scene I:

  At Thanksgiving time, J. B., his wife Sarah, and
their five children gather at the table. J. B., happy and
prosperous, obviously has much to be thankful for; in fact,
Sarah is afraid that God will take away their happiness unless they are deserving. J. B. tells her that no one can
deserve His blessings, for His gifts are freely bestowed.

Scene II:

  Nickles sneeringly declares that when J. B. loses
all his blessings, he will leave off praising God. Mr. Zuss
insists he will not.

Scene III:

  Two soldiers come and tell J. B. and Sarah that their
son has been killed in the war.

Scene IV:

  Two more of J. B.'s children perish in an automobile
accident. Although Sarah is growing more despairing, J. B.
does not turn from God.

Scene V:

  J. B.'s youngest daughter is raped and murdered,
but J. B. says "The Lord gives and the Lord taketh away."

Scene VI:

  J. B. loses his last child and his business as well.
Sarah blames God for their misfortunes, but still J. B. does
not curse His name.

Scene VII:

  Nickles tells Mr. Zuss that the spectacle of J. B.
praising the God who has permitted his misery is disgusting.
When Zuss accuses him of being a bad loser, Nickles insists he has not yet lost. God, he says, will finally drive
J. B. too far and he will forsake Him.

Scene VIII:

J. B., now covered with sores, begs God to show him his guilt. Sarah insists that they were all innocent, but J. B. says that God, being just, would not punish him without cause. Finally, Sarah deserts him.

Scene IX:

Three "comforters" come to visit J. B.--a communist, a psychiatrist, and a clergyman--but none can satisfactorily explain J. B.'s suffering. After J. B. rejects all three, God speaks to him in a whirlwind.

Scene X:

Nickles, disgusted that J. B. never cursed his God, grumbles that God always wins. When Zuss explains that J. B. gets his wife back and has more children, Nickles is amazed, declaring that no man would voluntarily live his life over again, least of all J. B.

Scene XI:

Sarah returns and J. B. tells her "to blow on the coal of the heart" and make ready to begin again.

Theatre History and Popular Response:

J. B. was first staged by the School of Drama at Yale on April 2, 1958. After numerous alterations, the play was brought to Broadway. It opened at the ANTA Theatre on December 11, 1958, and ran for 364 performances. Most of the reviewers were awed by MacLeish's achievement. One called the play "one of the memorable works of the century as verse, as drama, and as spiritual inquiry"; another said the play "reached heights of poetry and performance seldom attempted in the history of the American theatre." For representative reviews, see: Commentary, August, 1958, pp. 183-184; Harpers, April, 1959, pp. 77-78; New Yorker, December 20, 1958, pp. 70-72; Theatre Arts, August, 1958, pp. 9-11.

Critical Reputation:

      Archibald MacLeish (1892-) was born in a suburb
of Chicago, was educated in private schools, and was graduated from Yale University and the Harvard Law School. He
practiced law for a time with a prestigious Boston firm but
left to devote himself to literature. After serving in World
War I, he lived abroad and was a member of the avant-
garde led by Ezra Pound and T. S. Eliot. He returned to
the United States in 1928. Until 1958 MacLeish's reputation
rested largely upon his poetry, for which he had won two
Pulitzer Prizes. With J. B., however, his reputation as
a dramatist was established; indeed, according to one critic,
J. B. was one of the few plays in recent times which deserved serious consideration. A full-length study of his
work which treats the play is Signi Falk's Archibald Mac-
Leish, 1965. Other discussions of the play can be found in:
Charles Bond's "J. B. Is Not Job," Bucknell Review, IX
(1961), 272-280; C. C. Campbell's "The Transformation of
Biblical Myth: MacLeish's Use of the Adam and Job Stories," in Myth and Symbol, ed. by Bernice Slote, 1963;
Sheldon Grebstein's "J. B. and the Problem of Evil," University of Kansas City Review, XXIX (1963), 253-261; Kenneth Hamilton's "The Patience of J. B.," Dalhousie Review,
XLI (1961), 32-39; Andrew MacLeish's "J. B. and the Critics," Modern Drama, II (1959), 224-230; Marion Montgomery's "On First Looking into Archibald MacLeish's J. B.,"
Modern Drama, II (1959), 231-242; Eleanor Sickels' "Mac-
Leish and the Fortunate Fall," American Literature, XXXV
(1963), 205-217; George L. Sherman's "J. B.: The Making
of a Myth," Encore, VI (1959), 26-30; and M. T. Thelen's
"J. B., Job, and the Biblical Doctrine of Man," Journal of
the Bible and Religion, XXVII (1959), 201-205.

RAISIN IN THE SUN

Characters:

      Ruth Younger   Joseph Asagai
      Travis Younger   George Murchison
      Walter Lee Younger (Brother)   Karl Lindner
      Beneatha Younger   Bobo
      Lena Younger (Mama)   Moving Men

Act I:

   In a crowded and dingy apartment on Chicago's South-
side, Lena Younger, a wise old Negress, anxiously observes
the disintegration of her family. Her daughter Beneatha is
bright and ambitious, but she denies the God Lena has served
for so long. Her son Walter Lee, resenting his job as a
white man's chauffeur, hungers after enough money to escape
the ghetto and "be somebody." When his mother and his
wife Ruth object to his scheme of investing in a liquor store
with his father's life insurance money, Walter Lee furiously
denounces them for their slave mentality and lack of faith in
him. Because Walter's obsessive desire for money has
caused a rift between them, Ruth, upon discovering she is
pregnant, plans to have an abortion to avoid bringing another
child into the troubled family. When Walter refuses to forbid it, Lena declares him a disgrace to his father's memory.
Their heritage, she reminds him, is one of hard work and
love for children.

Act II:

   To Ruth's delight and Walter's disgust, Lena invests
some of the money in a house in a white neighborhood. Ruth
and Lena believe the move will mean salvation for Walter
and Ruth's children, but Walter sees it as the end of his
chance to go into business. When Walter's desperate unhappiness makes Lena realize that his manhood requires a commanding position in the household, she turns over the rest
of the money to him, including a sum reserved for Beneatha's
medical school tuition. Secretly, he gives the money to his
partner in the liquor store venture who promptly absconds
with it.

Act III:

   The family has resigned itself to the loss of the money when Walter Lee tells them he plans to sell the new house
to a White Citizens Committee which offered them a handsome
profit to prevent their moving into the neighborhood. Lena,
Ruth, and Beneatha are appalled by his cynicism and lack of
pride. When the representative of the Committee arrives,
Walter has a change of heart and tells him that they cannot
accept the offer; in fact, they plan to move in that afternoon.
As the play ends, Lena, realizing that her son has at last
come into his manhood, walks around the deserted apartment
one last time.

Theatre History and Popular Response:

  A Raisin in the Sun opened at the Ethel Barrymore
Theatre on March 11, 1959, and ran for 530 performances.
The play, a landmark in Negro drama in America, was
warmly received by the critics. Most regarded it as an
honest piece of playwriting which did not descend to trickery,
sentimentality, or propaganda. It was, one said, "a beautiful, lovable play." For representative reviews, see: Catholic World, May, 1959, p. 159; Commentary, June, 1959,
pp. 527-530; Theatre Arts, May, 1959, pp. 22-23; Time,
March 23, 1959, p. 58.

Critical Reputation:

  Lorraine Hansberry (1930-1965) was born in Chicago,
the daughter of a prosperous real estate broker. She attended "Jim Crow" schools on Chicago's South Side, then
went to the University of Wisconsin for two years. She
tried her hand at painting, but abandoned it to write plays
and short stories. After moving to New York in 1950, she
worked at odd jobs but continued to write. Her first success, Raisin in the Sun was followed by The Sign in Sidney
Brustein's Window in 1964. These plays suggested a promising career, but Miss Hansberry's untimely death in 1965
cut short these hopes. For further information on her life
and work, see Biographical Encyclopedia and Who's Who of
the American Theatre, 1966. For discussions of Raisin in
the Sun, consult C. W. E. Bigsby's Confrontation and Commitment: A Study of Contemporary American Drama, 1959-
1966, 1968, pp. 156-161; and Kenneth Tynan's Curtains,
1961, pp. 306-309.

The Theatre Season of

1959-1960

The Pulitzer Prize Committee surprised Broadway observers this season by giving its award to a musical, Fiorello! Once again they passed up Lillian Hellman, but the Drama Critics gave Toys in the Attic the Circle Award. The Tony Award went to William Gibson's The Miracle Worker. Jack Gelber's The Connection won the Obie. Also in the running were The Tenth Man, The Andersonville Trial, A Loss of Roses, and The Best Man.

FIORELLO!

Characters:

Announcer	Frankie Scarpini
Fiorello	Mitzi
Neil	Florence
Morris	Mrs. Pomerantz
Mr. Lopez	Reporter
Mr. Zappatella	Two Men
Marie	Tough Man
Dora	Derby
Ben	Sophie
Ed Peterson	Thea
Five Players	Secretary
Seedy Man	Senator
Four Hecklers	Commissioner
Nina	Frantic
Floyd	Judge Carter

Act I:

In 1914, Fiorello LaGuardia, a young Greenwich Village lawyer with volcanic energy and an acute social conscience, decides to run for Congress. His friends try to discourage him, assuming that Tammany has his district

sewed up. Undaunted, Fiorello goes to see Ben Marino,
Republican leader of the district, who cynically agrees to
give him the nomination since no one else wants to run.
Shortly after, Fiorello takes up the cause of some striking
garment workers, and, to the dismay of his secretary Marie,
falls in love with Thea, one of the strikers. He wins the
election, but his whirlwind career in Congress is cut short
by his tour of duty in World War I.

Act II:

          Ten years later, as Fiorello is preparing to run for
mayor of New York against Jimmy Walker, The Tammany
machine plots to assassinate him. Although he escapes
death, Walker defeats him at the polls, and to add to his
unhappiness, his wife Thea dies. Three years later, however, after he has successfully fought the machine through
the courts, Fiorello, now married to the faithful Marie, is
about to meet Walker at the polls a second time.

Theatre History and Popular Response:

          Fiorello!--a "smash hit"--opened at the Broadhurst
Theatre on November 23, 1959, and ran for 796 performances. Most of the critics received it warmly, agreeing
that it was a smooth, professional job, joyous and unpre-
tentious; "not a brash and busting big musical, but it doesn't
try to be, " as one reviewer expressed it. For representative reviews, see: America, February 13, 1960, p. 594;
Life, January 18, 1960, p. 422; New Yorker, December 5,
1959, pp. 95-97; Saturday Review, December 12, 1959, pp.
26-27.

Critical Reputation:

          George Abbot (1889-   ), born at Forestville, N.Y.,
attended public schools and then a military academy. He
received a B.A. from the University of Rochester in 1911,
then studied under George Pierce Baker at Harvard. He
went to New York as an actor but soon became more interested in writing, producing and directing plays. Now the
dean of Broadway showmen, he has been responsible, on the
average, for two productions a season for forty years. Some
of his better known hits are Pal Joey (1940), Where's Charlie
(1948), Call Me Madam (1950), Pajama Game (1954), Damn

Yankees (1953), and A Funny Thing Happened on the Way to
the Forum (1962).   Further details about Abbot's life and
work are available in Current Biography, 1965, pp. 1-3.

Abbot's collaborator for Fiorello! was Jerome Weid-
man (1913-), who was born in New York City, attended
public schools, the City College of New York and graduated
from New York University.   He attended law school for a
time, quit, and held various odd jobs.   He began writing
short stories, then produced a successful movie, I Can Get
It For You Wholesale, in 1937.   Since that time, Mr. Weid-
man, an astonishingly prolific writer, has been a librettist,
essayist, T.V. dramatist, as well as a novelist and writer
of short stories.   For further details, see Current Biography, 1942, pp. 875-877.

Fiorello!, like most musicals, has attracted little
scholarly interest.

TOYS IN THE ATTIC

Characters:

Carrie Berniers	Julian Berniers
Anna Berniers	Lily Berniers
Gus	Taxi Driver
Albertine Prine	Three Moving Men
Henry Simpson	

Act I:

Two sisters, Carrie and Anna Berniers, both middle-
aged spinsters who live on dreams--dreams of their younger
brother Julian's success--wait anxiously to hear from him.
When his mother-in-law, Albertine Prine, tells them that
Julian has been in New Orleans for a week without notifying
them, the sisters are hurt and mystified.   When Julian does
finally appear, he is full of joy over some mysterious business deal and loaded with expensive but inappropriate presents
for Carrie and Anna.

Act II:

Lily, Julian's young wife who is obviously mad, tells
her mother that Julian has a mistress who is responsible for
his new found wealth.   Mrs. Prine learns that the woman, a

Mrs. Warkins, is a cousin of Henry, Mrs. Prine's Negro
chauffeur as well as her lover. Meanwhile, Anna and Carrie
quarrel bitterly about Julian. Anna strikes upon the truth
when she accuses Carrie of having harbored an incestuous
passion for him all these years.

Act III:

Lily, in her madness, calls Mr. Warkins, the husband
of Julian's mistress, and implores him to see that his wife
allows her one more year with Julian. Carrie, who could
have stopped the call, does nothing; in fact, she tells Lily,
who tells Warkins where Julian and the woman are. When
Julian, bleeding and without a cent, returns home, Carrie
does not tell him Lily was responsible for his exposure, but
Mrs. Prine shrewdly realizes that Carrie will someday use
the information to get rid of Lily. In the meantime, both
sisters are happy to have Julian dependent on them again.

Theatre History and Popular Response:

Toys in the Attic opened at the Hudson Theatre on
February 25, 1960, and ran for 556 performances. The New
York critics held sharply divergent views concerning the
play's merit. Some called it Hellman's "most hellishly hyp-
notic drama, " "a smackingly vigorous" experience in play-
going. Others noted flaws in the play's structure, and one
complained that the subject matter--the problems of a deca-
dent Southern family--was repugnant. For representative reviews, see: America, May 28, 1960, p. 323; New Republic,
March 14, 1960, p. 22; New Yorker, March 5, 1960, pp.
124-125; Saturday Review, March 12, 1960, pp. 71-72.

Critical Reputation:

For a brief introduction to the life and work of Lillian
Hellman, see the entry for 1940-1941. Discussions of Toys
in the Attic can be found in Winifred Dusenbury's book The
Theme of Loneliness in Modern American Drama, 1960; in
Walter Kerr's The Theatre in Spite of Itself, 1963, pp. 235-
238; and in John Gassner's Dramatic Soundings, 1968, pp.
481-482. A useful critical article is Jacob Adler's "Miss
Hellman's Two Sisters, " Educational Theatre Journal, XV
(1963), 112-117.

THE MIRACLE WORKER

Characters:

Doctor	Aunt
Captain Keller	James Keller
Kate Keller	Michael Anagnos
Helen Keller	Annie Sullivan
Percy	A Group of Children
Martha	Viney

Act I:

When Annie Sullivan, a 21-year-old Irish girl, blind herself until recently, comes to Tuscumbia, Alabama, as governess for Helen Keller, Captain and Mrs. Keller doubt that she can help. Helen, both blind and deaf since infancy, is more animal than child; in fact, her brother James thinks she is mentally defective and should be committed to an asylum. Annie, whose most obvious trait is determination, begins at once to teach the little savage the alphabet for the deaf by spelling it into the child's hand. Helen responds by hitting Annie in the mouth and breaking her tooth, and then locking her in her bedroom.

Act II:

When Annie, realizing that Helen needs discipline, tries to teach her some table manners, the child throws a tantrum. Annie orders the astonished family out of the room and then, after a pitched battle, subdues her. Captain Keller, annoyed by what he considers Annie's Yankee presumptuousness, wants her dismissed, but Mrs. Keller is happy to see a little progress. Finally, Captain Keller grudgingly agrees to let Annie take Helen away from the pitying and indulgent family for two weeks. Annie is afraid two weeks will not be long enough to teach Helen the crucial thing--that the words she knows how to spell stand for objects.

Act III:

When Annie and Helen return, the Kellers are delighted that Annie has taught the child to behave, but Annie feels defeated because Helen still has no idea what language is. Then the miracle occurs. Helen connects the symbol and the thing symbolized, and her prison house is unlocked.

Theatre History and Popular Response:

    The Miracle Worker, which was first produced on
CBS Television, opened at the Playhouse on October 19,
1959, and ran for 700 performances. The reviewers found
it absorbing and moving, although some complained that Gibson had failed to translate the play into the idiom of the
theatre. According to one, he exhibited a tendency to "drain
what is already dry." For representative reviews, see:
America, November 14, 1959, p. 217; New Republic, November 9, 1959, pp. 28-29; New Yorker, October 31, 1959, pp.
132-134; Theatre Arts, December, 1959, p. 14.

Critical Reputation:

    William Gibson (1914-), was born in New York and
educated in New York City public schools, at Townsend Harris Hall, and at City College. Poet, novelist, short story
writer, Gibson's first contribution to the theatre was Two
for the Seesaw in 1958. Another play, Dinny and the Witches,
failed off-Broadway. For further information on Gibson's
life, see Biographical Index and Who's Who of the American
Theatre, 1966. For a bibliography, see Tulane Drama Review, May 1960. Allan Lewis' American Plays and Playwrights, 1965, contains a general appraisal of Gibson's work.
For discussions of The Miracle Worker, consult Walter
Kerr's The Theatre in Spite of Itself, 1963, pp. 255-257;
Kenneth Tynan's Curtains, 1961, pp. 327-330; and Gerald
Weales' "The Video Boys on Broadway," Antioch Review,
XXII (1962), 216-218.

THE CONNECTION

Characters:

Jim Dunn	First Photographer
Jaybird	Second Photographer
Leach	Harry
Solly	Sister Salvation
Sam	Cowboy
Arnie	

Act I:

    A producer, Jim Dunn, brings together a group of

heroin addicts, intending for them to improvise a play. The
scenario, prepared by the playwright Jaybird, calls for each
of the addicts to speak an improvised solo piece, followed by
spontaneous jazz improvisations provided by four musicians
on stage. In addition, Dunn has arranged for the action to
be filmed by some photographers who are making a film on
drug addiction. The addicts, who sit waiting for "the connection" to show up with their supply of heroin, are: Leach,
"a queer without being queer"; Sam, a sleepy Negro who believes that everyone is hooked on something and is trying to
make a connection; Solly, an intellectual Jew who only gets
a fix when he is happy; and Ernie, a psychopath with delusions of persecution. From time to time, Jaybird complains
that he is unable to control the scene or to achieve the effect he wants. Later, as the Cowboy, the connection, is
seen approaching, Dunn declares an intermission.

Act II:

        The Cowboy, a soft-spoken Negro, arrives, accompa-
nied by Sister Salvation, an elderly Salvation Army Sister who
has helped him elude the police. A turning-on celebration
follows. Even Jaybird and the photographers take heroin
for the first time. Leach takes an overdose and is revived
by the Cowboy. As the play ends, a character named Harry
comes in and, repeating an act he performed earlier in the
play, plugs a portable phonograph into an overhead connection, listens ecstatically to a Charlie Parker record, then
unplugs the machine and leaves.

Theatre History and Popular Response:

        The Connection opened at the Living Theatre on July
15, 1959, and ran for 678 performances. The first night
reviews were not particularly favorable, the consensus being
that the play was a "farrago of dirt." But the weekly reviewers kept the play alive until it caught on. For representative reviews, see: Harper, April 1960, pp. 26-28;
New Republic, September 28, 1959, pp. 29-30; Saturday Review, September 26, 1959, p. 27; New Yorker, October 10,
1959, pp. 126-129.

Critical Reputation:

        Jack Gelber (1932-), a native of Chicago, was edu-

cated at the University of Illinois (B.S. 1953), then spent
some time in a beatnik colony in San Francisco before going
to New York. He established himself as a playwright of
promise with The Connection, then followed it with The Apple
in 1961 and Square in the Eye, 1965. For further informa-
tion about his life, see Biographical Encyclopedia and Who's
Who of the American Theatre, 1966. For discussions of
The Connection, see Lionel Abel's "Not Everyone is in the
Fix," Partisan Review, XXVII (1960), 131-136; C. W. E.
Bigsby, Confrontation and Commitment, 1968, pp. 5, 50-61;
Robert Brustein's Seasons of Discontent, 1965, pp. 23-26;
Alan Downer's American Theatre Today, 1967, pp. 155-167;
Bernard Dukore's "The New Dramatists: Jack Gelber,"
Drama Survey, II (1962), 146-157; Stanley Eskin's "Theatri-
cality in the Avant-garde Drama," Modern Drama, VII (1964),
213-222; Walter Kerr's Theatre in Spite of Itself, 1963, pp.
182-185; Richard Kostelanetz's "The Connection: Heroin as
Existential Choice," Texas Quarterly, V (1962), 159-162;
Gerald Weales' American Drama Since World War II, 1962,
p. 203-223; and his The Jumping-Off Place: American Drama
in the 1960's, 1969, pp. 54-62; George Wellwarth's Theatre
of Protest and Paradox, 1964, pp. 293-295.

The Theatre Season of

1960-1961

Both the Pulitzer Prize and the Drama Critics' Circle Award went to Tad Mosel's play All the Way Home, based on James Agee's novel A Death in the Family. Foreign imports captured the Tony and the Obie Awards: the former went to Jean Anouilh's Becket, the latter to Jean Genet's The Blacks. Also running were Period of Adjustment; Mary, Mary; A Far Country; Big Fish, Little Fish; The Wall; and Advise and Consent.

ALL THE WAY HOME

Characters:

Rufus	Jim Wilson
Boys	Aunt Sadie Follet
Jay Follet	Great-Great-Granmaw
Mary Follet	Catherine Lynch
Ralph Follet	Aunt Hannah Lynch
Sally Follet	Joel Lynch
John Henry Follet	Andrew Lynch
Jessie Follet	Father Jackson

Act I:

In 1915, Jay and Mary Follet take their six-year-old son to visit Jay's Great-Great-Granmaw, aged 104. That night, Jay is summoned to the bedside of his father who has suddenly fallen ill. He and Mary part reluctantly, and Jay promises to be home in time for supper the next evening.

Act II:

The next day, Rufus goes shopping with his beloved Aunt Hannah, then goes home to wait for his father's return. Mary and her family, the Lynches, become concerned when Jay does not appear. Later that night, they receive word

161

that he has been in an accident. Mary's brother goes to see
about him and returns with the news that Jay is dead.

Act III:

  Rufus, who has not fully grasped the fact of his father's death, tries to get the attention of the neighborhood
boys by bragging that his father was killed in an auto accident. Mary, shattered by Jay's death, asks Jay's brother
if Jay, a reformed alcoholic, had been drinking, but Ralph
refuses to say. Mary finally accepts the fact that although
she and Jay loved each other, there was a side of Jay's
character that she would never understand. After the funeral,
Mary comforts Rufus and finds the courage to tell him about
the baby she is carrying.

Theatre History and Popular Response:

  When All the Way Home opened at the Belasco Theatre on November 30, 1960, the closing notices were posted
almost immediately. Critics complained that the play lacked
strength and unity, but nearly all were moved by its honesty
and simplicity. Finally, due to the tenacity of its producers
and the vocal support of its devotees, the play survived and
ran for 334 performances. For representative reviews, see:
America, January 14, 1961, p. 480; Life, January 27, 1961,
pp. 93-94; New Yorker, December 10, 1960, p. 96; Time,
December 12, 1960, p. 76.

Critical Reputation:

  Tad Mosel (1922-), was born at Steubenville, Ohio,
but moved with his family to the East when he was fourteen.
He received a B.A. from Amherst in 1947, then studied at
the Yale School of Drama and took the M.A. in drama at
Columbia in 1953. Although he had written prolifically and
successfully for television, contributing plays to such programs as Omnibus, Studio One and NBC Playhouse, Mosel
had never written a Broadway play before Fred Coe, the
producer, asked him to adapt Agee's autobiographical novel
for the stage. For further information about Mosel's life,
see Current Biography, 1961. To date, All the Way Home
has not received much scholarly attention.

The Theatre Season of

1961-1962

The Pulitzer Prize this season went to a musical, How to Succeed in Business Without Really Trying, written by Abe Burrows, Jack Weinstock, and Willie Gilbert. Tennessee Williams won the Circle Award for his Night of the Iguana. The Tony Award was captured by a British import, Robert Bolt's chronicle play, A Man for All Seasons. The Obie Award for Best American Play went to Frank Gilroy's Who'll Save the Plowboy? Also running were: Gideon; Oh Dad, Poor Dad, Mama's Hung You in the Closet and I'm Feeling So Sad; A Thousand Clowns; and Purlie Victorious.

The 1961-62 season also saw the beginning of a new award, The Burlington (Iowa) Players' Workshop Award, included here because it is typical of many prizes given for drama outside the New York area. According to the contest director, the aim of the Burlington contest was to find plays of literary worth and sound stage principles, plays which would be suitable for the commercial theatre. The winners received a cash prize and an opportunity to see their plays performed on the stage, usually during the season following the award. The judges, a literary agent, a director, and a noted teacher and critic of drama, chose Children of the Center Ring by Gerald Sanford as the first recipient of the prize.

HOW TO SUCCEED IN BUSINESS
WITHOUT REALLY TRYING

Characters:

Finch	Miss Jones
Gatch	Mr. Twinkle
Jenkins	Hedy
Tackaberry	Scrubwomen

Peterson   Mrs. Krumholtz
J. B. Biggley   Toynbee
Rosemary   Ovington
Bratt   Policeman
Smitty   Womper
Frump   Singers and Dancers

Act I:

J. Pierrepont Finch, an ambitious young window washer, reads a book entitled How to Succeed in Business Without Really Trying and decides to put its suggestions into practice. He gets a position in the mailroom of World Wide Wickets, Inc., then, by ingratiating himself to the right people, is promoted first to Junior Executive, then to Head of Promotions, then to Vice-President in charge of Advertising.

Act II:

Faced with the necessity of coming up with a brilliant promotional scheme, Finch, on a suggestion planted by his competitor Bud Frump (who has the advantage of being the president's nephew), tries to sell the president, J. B. Biggley, on a T.V. Treasure Hunt. Biggley is won over to the idea when Finch has Biggley's beautiful mistress, Hedy La-Rue, made the T.V. Treasure Girl. The show proves a disaster and Finch is on the verge of being fired when Mr. Womper, Chairman of the Board and an old window washer himself, takes Finch under his wing. Bud is fired when Womper learns he is Biggley's nephew, Womper retires and marries Hedy LaRue, and Finch, now married to Rosemary, a pretty secretary who has helped him move swiftly up the ladder of success, becomes Chairman of the Board.

Theatre History and Popular Response:

How to Succeed opened at the 46th Street Theatre on October 14, 1961, and had a long run of 1,417 performances. The reviewers turned in laudatory reviews, calling the show "a brilliant musical comedy," and describing it as "gay, zingy, amoral, witty and shot with style." One said it "belongs to the bluechips among modern musicals." For representative reviews, see: Commonweal, November 3, 1961, p. 154; National Review, January 16, 1962, pp. 31-33; New Republic, November 6, 1961, p. 23; Theatre Arts, December, 1961, pp. 8-9.

Critical Reputation:

Abe Burrows, (1910-), the principal contributor to
How to Succeed, was born in New York City and educated in
the public schools.   He attended City College as a pre-med
student until he abandoned his studies and pursued odd jobs.
He has been a nightclub comedian, a free-lance radio writer,
a radio performer, a "play doctor," and is co-author of the
successful musical Guys and Dolls.

Although Burrows got most of the credit for the show,
Jack Weinstock (1909-1969) and Willie Gilbert (1916-), both
television writers, were the first to see the possibilities of
dramatizing Shepherd Mead's 1962 book, How to Succeed in
Business Without Really Trying: A Dastard's Guide to Fame
and Fortune.   Jack Weinstock, a practicing urologist, was
born in New York City and studied at Columbia and Bellevue
Medical School.   Willie Gilbert was born in Cleveland, Ohio,
was educated in public schools, and received a B.S. from
the Ohio State University in 1938.   He began his career by
writing variety shows for television.   He and Weinstock
wrote Hot Spot, a musical comedy, in 1963.   For further information on the three collaborators, consult Biographical
Encyclopedia and Who's Who of the American Theatre, 1966.
How to Succeed has been shown little interest by scholars.

NIGHT OF THE IGUANA

Characters:

Maxine Faulk	Wolfgang
Pedro	Hilda
Pancho	Judith Fellows
Reverend Shannon	Hannah Jelkes
Hank	Charlotte Goodall
Herr Fahrenkopf	Jonathan Coffin (Nonno)
Frau Fahrenkopf	Jake Latte

Act I:

In 1940, the Rev. T. Lawrence Shannon, inactive in
the ministry since he was locked out of his church for im-
morality and heresy, is now reduced to acting as a guide
for a third-rate tour company.   He brings a busload of
teachers from a Baptist female college in Texas to Puerto
Barrio, Mexico.   Shannon, feeling himself near collapse,

wants to stay overnight at the Costa Verde Hotel, run by his
friends Fred and Maxine Faulk. The women, however, want
to go on and refuse to get out of the bus. Shannon is afraid
the women will have him fired (he is in particularly bad
graces for allowing himself to be seduced by a young girl in
the party), but he cannot bring himself to go on. Upon ar-
riving at the hotel, he discovers that Fred has died recently.
The lusty Maxine, who has always admired Shannon, begs
him to give up the tour and move in with her. Meanwhile,
Hannah Jelkes, a New England spinster of about 40, arrives
at the Costa Verde with her ninety-two-year-old grandfather,
Nonno, "the world's oldest living and practicing poet." They
have been around the world many times, but they have no
money. Maxine, sensing Shannon's immediate attraction to
Hannah, wants to turn them away, but Hannah, a painter, insists that she and her grandfather will earn their keep with
their pictures and poetry. Maxine, at Shannon's urging,
grudgingly consents.

Act II:

Shannon, still being pursued by Charlotte, the girl he
succumbed to on the trip, is afraid that his emotional re-
serves are too low for any involvements and runs away from
her. Later that evening he tells Hannah about his career in
the Church, his failures, his fears. Maxine falls into a
jealous rage when she realizes the sympathetic relationship
that has sprung up between Hannah and Shannon. She reacts
violently and they quarrel bitterly.

Act III:

When the touring company sends a man to take over
the bus, Shannon breaks down and runs away, threatening to
swim out into the ocean. Maxine has him caught and tied
up, and Hannah watches over him through the night. After
he calms down, Hannah unties him. He then unties a giant
lizard, an iguana, that Maxine's Mexican boys have captured,
a creature, like Shannon, at the end of its rope. In spite
of her sympathy and respect for Shannon, Hannah rejects his
suggestion that they become lovers or travel together. Later,
Shannon accepts Maxine's offer to stay and help her run the
Costa Verde. Meanwhile, Nonno finishes his last poem--his
loveliest--and dies quietly. Hannah makes plans to go on
alone.

Theatre History and Popular Response:

Night of the Iguana opened at the Royale Theatre on December 28, 1961, and ran for 316 performances. Some reviewers hailed it as Williams' best play, an "awesome and powerful" work, as one called it. Others, while conceding its moving theatrical qualities, observed that the play lacked action and was basically undramatic. According to one critic, it "shoots off a lot of sparks, but few catch fire." For representative reviews, see: America, February 3, 1962, p. 604; Commonweal, January 26, 1962, p. 460; Nation, January 27, 1962, p. 86; Theatre Arts, March, 1962, p. 57.

Critical Reputation:

A brief introduction to Tennessee Williams' life and art can be found under the entry for 1944-1945. The full-length studies of his plays cited there contain discussions of Night of the Iguana. For further critical discussion of the play, see Robert Brustein's Seasons of Discontent, 1965, pp. 126-129; Walter Kerr's The Theatre In Spite of Itself, 1963, pp. 247-255; and Gerald Weales' The Jumping-Off Place, 1969, pp. 5-7. Jacob Adler's "Night of the Iguana: A New Tennessee Williams?" Ramparts, I (November, 1962), 59-68, is a provocative critical article.

WHO'LL SAVE THE PLOWBOY?

Characters:

Albert Cobb	The Doctor
Helen Cobb	The Man
Larry Doyle	The Boy
Mr. Doyle	

Act I:

When Larry Doyle goes to see Albert Cobb, an army buddy whose life he saved fifteen years earlier, the Cobbs wonder about his motive. Albert hopes Larry has come to offer him a job, but Helen, Albert's despondent, quarrelsome wife, suspects the old friend of wanting to sell them something. Larry, after a joyous reunion with Albert, explains that he merely came to see if Albert and his family are happy. They assure him that they are, but when Larry inquires

about little Larry, his namesake, the couple give evasive
answers. Later that night after Helen has retired, Albert
confesses that he has failed at everything he has attempted,
that he and Helen are wretchedly unhappy together, and that
liquor and casual sexual encounters are all that keep him
going. Larry, horrified by the disclosure, tries to leave
but collapses on the stairs. Albert and Helen summon a
doctor and then Larry's mother. Mrs. Doyle tells Albert
that Larry is dying of the wound he received while saving
Albert and implores him to convince Larry that he is successful and happy. Otherwise, Larry will die knowing that
he gave his life for nothing.

Act II:

        The next day while Albert is out, Larry learns that
Helen has a lover. He also discovers that the boy Larry
was born deformed and is confined to an institution. Bitterly, Helen tells Larry that Albert was not worth saving,
and she confesses that they know about his fatal illness.
When Albert arrives with a boy he has coached to play the
part of young Larry, Larry goes along with the ruse, then
leaves. Albert is never aware that Larry knew the truth.

Theatre History and Popular Response:

        Who'll Save the Plowboy? opened at the Phoenix Thea-
tre on January 8, 1962, and ran for 46 performances. The
critics were divided in their reaction to the play. One or
two simply dismissed it as deplorable; most, however, conceded that even though it was obviously a "journeyman ef-
fort," it had its moments of "power, sincerity, and truth."
One called it "a gritty and gripping play." For representative reviews, see Educational Theatre Journal, March, 1962,
p. 72; National Review, February 5, 1962, pp. 29-30; The
Reporter, March 1, 1962, p. 48; Theatre Arts, March,
1962, p. 61.

Critical Reputation:

        Frank Gilroy (1929-) was born in New York City,
studied in the public schools, and attended Dartmouth where
he received the B.A. in 1950. He studied playwriting for a
year at the Yale School of Drama, then began his career by
writing for such television shows as Playhouse 90, Studio One,

U.S. Steel Hour, Omnibus and the Kraft Theatre. His successes in television gave him the leisure to try his hand at
serious plays. He made his theatre debut with Who'll Save
the Plowboy? He followed this auspicious beginning with a
prize-winning play, The Subject Was Roses (see entry for
1964-1965). Two of his recent plays are That Summer--That
Fall (1967), a retelling of the Phaedra legend, and The Only
Game in Town (1968), a comedy. For further information
on Gilroy's life and career, see Current Biography, 1965.
Gerald Weales discusses Who'll Save the Plowboy? in The
Jumping-Off Place, 1969, p. 86.

CHILDREN OF THE CENTER RING

Characters:

Evan	Alfredo
Mauve	Hugo
Mother	

Act I:

When Alfredo, a celebrated aerialist, retires after a
fall, he vows he will recover and return to the circus. His
children, Evan and Mauve, both secretly hope he will always be a cripple. Evan resents his father's international
reputation, and Mauve resents his independence and thirst
for life. Evan insists that he hates circus life, but when
Alfredo's friend Hugo, fifty years a clown, offers to teach
Evan his act, the boy agrees, hoping to achieve an even
greater fame than Alfredo's.

Act II:

Alfredo polishes his medals, savors his memories,
and exercises four hours a day to speed his recovery.
Evan, irritated by his father's bragging, calls him a dead
man who clings to the relics of his past. Alfredo counters
by saying that Evan will never be the man that he is. When
Evan puts on his first clown performance for the family,
Alfredo's presence unnerves him. Evan performs badly,
then, humiliated and enraged, he knocks his father to the
floor and runs away.

Act III:

Hugo tells Alfredo's wife that Alfredo is responsible for Evan's misery. He claims that Alfredo cared only for the applause of strangers, but did not bother to earn his son's respect. When Evan returns, he tells his mother that he hates Alfredo for the way he has neglected her and run after other women. The mother confesses that loving Alfredo and existing in his shadow was all the life she wanted. Evan, dismayed at the intensity of Mother's passion, tells her he is leaving home for good. The next morning, Alfredo has a talk with Mauve and tries to explain that he was unaware of his children's unhappiness. He also tells her that he will never succumb to being an invalid; in fact, he feels stronger and better than ever. Mauve challenges him to prove his strength by swinging from the fire escape. When Alfredo plunges to his death, Mauve tells Evan that the eagle has at last fallen from the sky.

Theatre History:

Children of the Center Ring was presented by the Players' Workshop of Burlington, Iowa, April 25-28, 1963. Sanford later rewrote the play for television.

Critical Reputation:

Gerald Sanford, a native of St. Louis, Missouri, did not attend college but did study for three months at the American Theatre Wing School. After he decided on a career as a writer, he had one play produced off-Broadway, then turned his attention to writing television scripts. He has had his work accepted by such programs as Dr. Kildare, Empire, Mr. Novak and The Kraft Theatre.

The Theatre Season of

1962-1963

The play of the season was Edward Albee's searing
Who's Afraid of Virginia Woolf? which took both the Drama
Critics' Award and the Tony Award. The Pulitzer jurors
recommended the play, but the Advisory Board overruled
them and withheld the Prize, a timid gesture which caused
jurors John Mason Brown and John Gassner to resign in disgust. No Obie award for Best Play was given this season.
Passed over were: The Milk Train Doesn't Stop Here Any
More; Natural Affection; Never Too Late; Lorenzo; My Mother, My Father, and Me. The Players' Workshop Award
went to Vincent Longhi's comedy, Climb the Greased Pole.

WHO'S AFRAID OF VIRGINIA WOOLF?

Characters:

  Martha   Nick
  George   Honey

Act I: Fun and Games

When George, a professor of history, and his wife
Martha, the university president's daughter, come home rather drunk from a faculty party, they begin a slashing quarrel
in which Martha calls George a dullard and a weakling, and
he calls her a braying exhibitionist. The fight goes on in
spite of the arrival of Nick, a newcomer to the biology faculty, and his wife Honey. Upset by the quarrel and especially
by Martha's strident vulgarity, they try to leave, but Martha
and George will not hear of it, and sparring continues with
Martha the aggressor. To Nick and Honey's acute discom-
fort, Martha explains that George, once thought presidential
timbre by her father, is bogged down in the history department. George counters by saying that Martha is a drunkard
and a bad mother to their twenty-one-year-old son.

Act II: Walpurgisnacht

Martha finally goads George until he attempts to
strangle her. After Nick rescues her, the first game--
"Get the Host"--comes to an end. George, still smarting
from his humiliation at Martha's hands, begins a new game--
"Get the Guests." Under the guise of relating the plot of
his latest novel, George reveals what Nick had told him earlier about Honey: that she was the daughter of a rich but
dishonest preacher whom he married because she had a false
pregnancy. Martha, appalled at George's vicious assault on
the defenseless Honey, declares no holds barred and encourages Nick to make love to her. George establishes the elab-
orate pretense that he does not care. Honey, meanwhile,
has passed out on the bathroom floor.

Act III: Exorcism

When Martha and Nick reappear, she heaps scorn upon him for his sexual inadequacy and reveals that George,
in spite of her need to torment and shame him, is the only
man she loves and the only one who satisfies her physically.
George comes in and insists that Nick and Honey, whom they
have to revive, play one last game--"Bringing Up Baby."
Martha begs piteously that he not discuss their son, but
George is adamant. Together they relate the story of his
growing up, each accusing the other of failure as a parent.
Finally, George tells Martha that the boy has been killed in
an accident. It soon becomes clear that the son is an imag-
inary one, "killed off" by George because Martha's earlier
references to him were against the rules of their game.
After Honey and Nick leave, George and Martha, now strangely at peace, contemplate the future without their delusions.

Theatre History and Popular Response:

Who's Afraid of Virginia Woolf?, which opened at the
Billy Rose Theatre on October 13, 1962, and ran for 664
performances, was one of the most controversial Broadway
plays in years. The critics were sharply divided in their
opinion of the play's merit. Some spoke of it in glowing
terms, calling it "the most shattering drama ... since
O'Neill's Long Day's Journey Into Night," and a play of
"energy and distinction." Others thought it too savage. One
reviewer, for example, said it was "four characters wide
and a cesspool deep." Another considered it "obsessively

vulgar, unnecessarily obscene, too drawn out, and not ideally
resolved." For representative reviews, see: Nation, October 27, 1962, pp. 273-274; New Republic, November 3, 1962,
pp. 29-30; Newsweek, October 29, 1962, p. 52; Saturday Review, October 27, 1962, p. 29.

Critical Reputation:

        Edward Albee (1928-) was adopted as an infant by
a wealthy family with theatre connections. He studied at
several private schools and briefly attended Trinity College.
In 1950 he left home, held odd jobs, and wrote poetry, fiction and plays. The first public recognition of his work
came when his one-act play The Zoo Story (1959) was produced in Berlin and then brought to an off-Broadway theatre.
Since that time, he has established himself as one of America's most promising playwrights with such plays as The
Death of Bessie Smith (1961), The Sandbox (1960), The
American Dream (1961), all one-acts. Virginia Woolf was
his first full-length play; he followed it with Ballad of the
Sad Cafe (1963), Tiny Alice (1964), Malcolm (1966), A Delicate Balance, the Pulitzer Prize winner for 1966-1967, and
Everything in the Garden (1967). His most recent works
are Box (1968), Quotations from Chairman Mao (1968), and
All Over (1971).

        Current Biography, 1963, contains a sketch of Albee's
life and work. For full length studies of his art, see Gilbert Debuscher's Edward Albee: Tradition and Renewal,
1967; Richard Anacher's Edward Albee, 1969; Ruby Cohn's
Edward Albee, 1969; and Michael Rutenberg's Edward Albee:
Playwright in Protest, 1969.

        Who's Afraid of Virginia Woolf? has also been the
subject of numerous critical articles: C. W. E. Bigsby's
"Curiouser and Curiouser: Edward Albee and the Great God
Reality," Modern Drama, X (1967), 258-266; and his "Who's
Afraid of Virginia Woolf? : Edward Albee's Morality Play,"
Journal of American Studies, I (1967), 257-268; D. E. Cole-
man's "Fun and Games: Two Pictures of Heartbreak House,"
Drama Survey, V (1966-1967), 223-236; Earl Dias's "Full-
Scale Albee," Drama Critique, VIII (1965), 107-112; Richard
Dozier's "Adultery and Disappointment in Who's Afraid of
Virginia Woolf?," Modern Drama, II (1969), 432-436; B. F.
Dukore's "A Warp in Albee's Woolf," Southern Speech Jour-
nal, XXX (1964), 261-268; Arthur Evans' "Love, History,

and Edward Albee, " Renascence, XIX (1967), 115-118; Joy
Flasch's "Games People Play in Who's Afraid of Virginia
Woolf?", Modern Drama, X (1967), 280-288; Wendell Har-
ris' "Morality, Absurdity, and Albee, " Southwest Review,
XLIX (1964), 249-256; Charles Lyons' "Some Variations of
'Kindermord' as Dramatic Archetype, " Comparative Drama,
I (1967), 56-71; Daniel McDonald's "Truth and Illusion in
Who's Afraid of Virginia Woolf?", Renascence, XVII (1964),
63-69; Ruth Meyer's "Language: Truth and Illusion in Who's
Afraid of Virginia Woolf?", English Theatre Journal, XX
(1968), 60-69; Louis Paul's "A Game Analysis of Albee's
Who's Afraid of Virginia Woolf?", Literature and Psychology,
XVII (1967), 47-51; Emil Roy's "Who's Afraid of Virginia
Woolf? and The Tradition, " Bucknell Review, XIII (1965),
27-36; Richard Schechner's "Who's Afraid of Edward Albee?",
Tulane Drama Review, VII (1963), 7-10; Alan Schneider's
"Why So Afraid?", Tulane Drama Review, VII (1963), 10-13;
Marion Taylor's "Edward Albee and August Strindberg: Some
Parallels Between The Dance of Death and Who's Afraid of
Virginia Woolf?", Papers on English Language and Litera-
ture, I (1965), 59-71; and Diana Trilling's "The Riddle of
Albee's Who's Afraid of Virginia Woolf?", Claremont Es-
says, 1964, pp. 203-227.

CLIMB THE GREASED POLE

Characters:

Charlie Hacker	Bishop Corelli
Kathleen Hacker	Tony Mulcahy
Peggy Hacker	Ambulance Doctor
Alfie Mulcahy	Mrs. Verde
Angie Mulcahy	Mrs. O'Brien
Niko	Mrs. Butacavoli

Act I:

Kathleen Hacker, a devout Catholic, has bought a
five-foot, 105-pound cheese which she plans to donate as a
prize in the Climb-the-Greased-Pole Contest, an annual event
at the St. Anthony's Day Celebration in her parish.   When
her husband Charlie, a militant atheist, comes home and
sees the "stinking totem pole, " he explodes and accuses her
of breaking her oath not to practice her religion openly at
home until their daughter Peggy leaves the nest.   He complains that all Kathleen cares about is the next world when

what he wants is a chance to take a trip and see this one.
When she points out that his picture of Einstein, his copy of
Darwin's Origin of the Species, and his telescope are the
symbols of his religion, he accuses her of trying to coerce
him into marrying her in the Church because she thinks they
have been living in sin since their civil ceremony. Peggy,
sick of Charlie's bullying of Kathleen, announces that she is
moving out, leaving Kathleen free to be as Catholic as she
likes.

Act II:

    Kathleen immediately installs holy pictures and statues
on her side of the living room, and the objects which Charlie
venerates he moves to the other. Charlie, unnerved by Kathleen's triumph, consoles himself by drinking heavily with his
friend Alfie. Alfie, unbeknownst to Charlie and Kathleen, is
an ex-monk who, when intoxicated, begins to celebrate imag-
inary church services. When the ladies of the St. Anthony's
Feast Day Committee come to give Kathleen the "Religious
Wife of the Year" Award, the drunken Alfie, to everyone's
horror, goes into his act. When Kathleen confesses to the
outraged churchwomen that she has never been married in
the church, they storm out.

Act III:

    Kathleen packs to leave, tearfully complaining that
Charlie has never made one sacrifice for her. He decides
to attempt the greased pole, falls, and is carried home unconscious. While Kathleen is delivering a fervent prayer to
St. Anthony on his behalf, he revives, and asks Kathleen to marry him in church. The happy couple plan to leave for a
second honeymoon in Rome; the prize is reawarded to Kathleen by the Ladies' Committee because they can find no one
more deserving than Kathleen.

Theatre History:

    Climb the Greased Pole was presented by the Players'
Workshop, December 5 through 8, 1963. The play, a doc-
tored version of the playwright's boyhood experiences, was
subsequently given a prestigious production at the Mermaid
Theatre in London. It received mixed reviews, but was
published and has since played around the English speaking
world--even in Tasmania. Mr. Longhi is still hoping for a

New York production.

Critical Reputation:

        Vincent Longhi, lawyer and playwright, was born and
reared in a tough waterfront section of New York City.   His
first play, Two Fingers of Pride, was produced off-Broadway.   Mr. Longhi takes pride in having started his career
with the play in which Steve McQueen made his acting debut.
The playwright has subsequently moved to London with his
family where he writes plays and television specials for the
B. B. C.

The Theatre Season of

1963-1964

The Pulitzer Prize was not awarded again this season.
Both the Circle and the Tony Awards went to Luther by the
British playwright John Osborne. The Obie Award for Best
American Play went to Dutchman by LeRoi Jones. Passed
over were: After the Fall; The Passion of Joseph D.; Bare-
foot in the Park; The Ballad of the Sad Cafe; and Any Wednes-
day. The third annual Players' Workshop Award went to
Paul T. Nolan for his play There's Death for the Lonely.

DUTCHMAN

Characters:

    Clay   Riders of Coach,
    Lula   black and white
    Young Negro   Conductor

Scene I:

      Lula, an attractive white woman, boards a subway
and sits down by a well-dressed young Negro named Clay.
She smiles seductively at him and then engages him in con-
versation. Clay, a poet, is fascinated by her manner which
is alternately suggestive and insulting. She invites him to
spend the evening with her, then twits him for lusting after
middle-class respectability in the white man's world.

Scene II:

      Lula finally enrages Clay, who delivers a savage
speech in which he confesses his murderous hatred for her
and for all white people. Calmly she stabs him, then gets
the passengers to throw his body off the train. Everyone
leaves the car but Lula who sits alone until another young
black man boards the car. The play ends as she gives him
the same seductive smile she had given Clay.

177

Theatre History and Popular Response:

     Dutchman opened at the Cherry Lane Theatre on
March 24, 1964, on the same program with Fernando Arra-
bal's Two Executioners and Samuel Beckett's Play. It continued its run with Edward Albee's The American Dream.
Altogether, the play was performed 366 times. It was, for
the most part, well received, with reviewers applauding its
"raw power" and "explosive violence." Jones was proclaimed
a "turbulent talent" whose message Americans badly needed
to hear. One reviewer called Dutchman "the most impressive work by an American playwright in the last few years."
For representative reviews, see: Nation, April 13, 1964,
pp. 383-384; Newsweek, April 13, 1964, p. 60; New Yorker,
April 4, 1964, pp. 78-79; Vogue, July 1964, p. 32.

Critical Reputation:

     LeRoi Jones (1934-), was born in Newark, New
Jersey, and received his education at the Newark branch of
Rutgers University and Howard University. Jones, a poet,
novelist, teacher, and political activist, is one of the founders of black revolutionary drama in America. His plays
after Dutchman--The Toilet (1964), The Slave (1964), Black
Mass (1964), Madheart (1967), and Great Goodness of Life
(1967)--mark him as an angry black separatist who sees no
hope for the assimilation of the Negro in American life
(which he sees as sterile and culturally bankrupt). In an
attempt to foster black nationalism, Jones, under the name
of Imamu Amiri Baraka, founded the Black Arts Repertory
Theatre in Harlem and also the Spirit House in Newark.
For discussions of Dutchman, see C. W. E. Bigsby's Confrontation and Commitment (1968); Hugh Nelson's "LeRoi
Jones' Dutchman: A Brief Ride on a Doomed Ship," Educational Theatre Journal, XX (March, 1968), 53-59; and Gerald
Weales' The Jumping-Off Place, 1969, pp. 134-147. See also the Tulane Drama Review, XII (Summer, 1968), the entire issue of which is devoted to Black Theatre.

THERE'S DEATH FOR THE LONELY

Characters:

Mr. Gates	Faye Allen
Mrs. Clyme	Duke Taylor

Donne   Amos Rogers
Houseman   Loretta Grant
Duchess Britt   Billy Joe Jenkins
Sabre Dawson

Act I:

At his isolated mansion on an island near the coast
of the United States, a sinister host, Mr. Gates, has just
collected the latest group of victims for a macabre game he
plays. His guests, who have only their loneliness in common, include Mrs. Allen, a runaway housewife; Miss Dawson, a career woman; Miss Britt, an alcoholic spinster;
Duke Taylor, a drifter; Amos Rogers, a middle-aged bachelor; Loretta Grant, a young black schoolteacher; and Billy
Joe Jenkins, a displaced Southerner. Gates has lured them
into the game by promising each something he wants badly,
but once the bargain is struck, he reveals the terms. The
guests are to vote each Sunday to select the loneliest one in
the group. The final winner's prize will be death.

Act II:

At first the victims instinctively cling together. Mrs.
Allen and Miss Dawson form what the others consider a rather unwholesome alliance; Jenkins and Miss Grant seek each
other out; and Rogers unites the men in an escape plot.
Only Miss Britt, who moves about in an alcoholic fog, is
alone. When Rogers' plot backfires and Taylor accidentally
kills Miss Grant instead of Gates, the lonely begin to quarrel and to harbor suspicion and resentment. After the failure of his plan, Rogers kills himself. The rest use the bal-
lot to revenge themselves upon each other.

Act III:

On the last night, Taylor is chosen the loneliest. He
accuses Jenkins of plotting against him. When the angry
Jenkins retaliates with a threatening gesture at Taylor, one
of Gates' henchmen shoots him, leaving only Mrs. Allen,
Miss Dawson, Taylor, and Miss Britt to vote. Miss Britt
votes for herself and urges Taylor to vote for her as well.
She wins the deadly game and is taken away. Taylor and the
two women are released. As the play ends, Gates and his
cohorts discuss the next game. He tells them he plans to
have some hack writer do a play about lonely people. Gates
will stand outside the theatre and select his next group from

the audience.

Theatre History:

There's Death for the Lonely was given its premier
performance by the Burlington Players on December 13
through 16, 1964.   The play, subsequently revised and published by Edgemoor Press, was reviewed in Dramatics, May,
1971, p. 10.   Nolan relates his experience as the prize-win-
ner in "One Step to Broadway," Dramatics, February, 1967,
p. 15, and discusses the history of the play in "From Script
to Stage," Janus, March, 1972, pp. 34-35.

Critical Reputation:

Paul T. Nolan (1919-   ) was born in Rochester, New
York, studied at private schools; received the Ph.D. at
Tulane University (1953); and is presently Dupré Professor
of Humanities at the University of Southwestern Louisiana.
Nolan is essentially a teacher who writes rather than a professional playwright.   James Salem, in his thesis-anthology,
The Teacher as Writer: Paul T. Nolan, Example, 1970,
suggests that for Nolan the printed page and the stage are
largely extensions of the classroom, an observation that is
probably less true of Death for the Lonely than of his other
works.   Beverly Matherne in a bibliographical essay, "Louisiana Playwright: Paul T. Nolan," Louisiana Studies,
(March, 1972), 1-12, lists over eighty of Nolan's plays
which have been published one or more times.   Most of
these plays are intended for the academic theatre, primarily
the high school theatre, and include Round-the-World Plays,
Drama Workshop Plays, and Chaucer for Children, collections of one-act plays.

The Theatre Season of

1964-1965

This season The Subject Was Roses by Frank Gilroy captured the Pulitzer Prize, The Circle Award, and the Tony Award. The Obie went to Robert Lowell's verse play The Old Glory. Other plays in the running were Luv, The Odd Couple, Slow Dance on the Killing Ground, Incident at Vichy and Tiny Alice. The fourth (and final) Players' Workshop Award went to Richard Stockton's One World at a Time.

THE SUBJECT WAS ROSES

Characters:

    John Cleary
    Nettie Cleary
    Timmy Cleary

Act I:

    When Timmy Cleary comes home after World War II, his parents, John and Nettie, try to conceal their hostilities toward each other, but almost immediately they engage in a struggle for the boy's affection. One afternoon Timmy impulsively buys roses for Nettie but persuades his father to pretend they were his idea. After Timmy goes to bed, Nettie tells John that the flowers made her feel tender toward him, but when he attempts to make love to her, she rebuffs him, reminding him of her grievances. Enraged, John tells her the roses were Timmy's idea.

Act II:

    The next day even more violent quarrels ensue. Nettie leaves home for twelve hours while John and Timmy anxiously wait for news of her. Her return, however, is only the occasion for more recriminations. By the next morning,

realizing that he must escape, Timmy announces he is leaving home. He manages, however, to tell his father that he
loves him. Although John wants the boy to stay, he realizes
that his presence will only exacerbate the trouble between
Nettie and himself, so when Timmy weakens for a moment
and says he will stay, John tells him they have already
made other plans for his room.

Theatre History and Popular Response:

        The Subject Was Roses opened at The Royale Theatre
on May 25, 1964, and ran for 832 performances. The reviews were, for the most part, favorable. Some complained
that the three characters were uninteresting and that the
play went nowhere, but most conceded that it was honest and
moving. For representative reviews, see: Nation, June 15,
1964, p. 611; New Yorker, June 6, 1964, p. 86; Saturday
Review, June 13, 1964, p. 44; Time, June 5, 1964, p. 75.

Critical Reputation:

        For a brief introduction to Gilroy's life and work,
see the entry for 1961-1962. John Gassner discusses The
Subject Was Roses in Dramatic Soundings, 1968, p. 578;
Gerald Weales treats it in The Jumping-Off Place, 1969,
pp. 85-90.

THE OLD GLORY

MY KINSMAN, MAJOR MOLINEUX

Characters:

Robin	Clergyman
Boy (his brother)	Prostitute
Ferryman	Colonel Greenough
1st Redcoat	Man in Periwig
2nd Redcoat	Watchman
First Barber	Major Molineux
Tavern Keeper	Citizens of Boston
Man with Pewter Mug	

        Shortly before the American Revolution, Robin, a boy
of eighteen, and his brother, a lad of ten, leave their home

in Deerfield to go to Boston. They expect to be under the
protection of their uncle, Major Molineux, the colonial governor. Upon reaching Boston, they ask various citizens
where they can find their kinsman, but each time they are
rudely repulsed, derided, or threatened. Finally, they see
Major Molineux, tarred and feathered, led in a parade by
the mysterious Colonel Greenough. Robin calls to his uncle,
but because the boy is holding a Rattlesnake flag, thrust into
his hand by someone in the crowd, the Major assumes that
Robin is part of the rebellion and cries, "Et tu, Brute."
After the mob kills Major Molineux, Robin, his great ex-
pectations dashed, decides to stay in Boston rather than return to the farm.

BENITO CERENO

Characters:

Captain Amasa Delano	Francesco
John Perkins	American Sailors
Don Benito Cereno	Spanish Sailors
Babu	Negro Slaves
Atufal	

        The play, set in about 1800, begins when Amasa
Delano, captain of The President Adams, an American sailing
vessel lying off the coast of Trinidad, sights a ship in dis-
tress. When he and his bosun, John Perkins, board The San
Domingo with food and water, they discover a cargo of slaves
who cry out piteously that scurvy, yellow fever, storms, fam-
ine and thirst have plagued them. Don Benito, the elegant
young captain, is so worn by hardship that he seems to take
little interest in running the ship. He is attended constantly
by Babu, an obsequious little Negro who hovers about him,
anticipating every need. Captain Delano, a naive and innocent man, finally realizes that the slaves, led by Babu, are
in command of the ship and are keeping Don Benito prisoner.
Just as the Negroes seize Delano and tell him to sail them to
Africa, men from The President Adams board the ship and
put down the rebellion. Babu confesses to having killed the
owner, Don Aranda. As Babu cries that the future is with
the black man, Delano shouts, "This is your future" and
empties his pistol into the slave's body.

Theatre History and Popular Response:

    The Old Glory was written by Robert Lowell as a
trilogy consisting of Endecott and the Red Cross, based on
two short stories by Nathaniel Hawthorne; My Kinsman,
Major Molineux, based on Hawthorne's story of the same
name; and Benito Cereno, from the Melville novella. The
three plays were a unit designed to illuminate, according to
Robert Brustein in his introduction to the published version
of the play, "the American character at three different points
in its historical development." But when The Old Glory
opened at the American Place Theatre on November 1, 1964,
Endecott and the Red Cross had been dropped. The Old
Glory only ran for 36 performances, partly because local
reviewers, according to Brustein, had been "predictably dull-
witted" about the play and had not turned in favorable reviews. On January 14, 1965, Benito Cereno opened at the
Theatre de Lys where it ran for 86 performances. For representative reviews, see: Nation, November 23, 1964, pp.
390-391; New Republic, November 21, 1964, p. 28; New
Yorker, November 14, 1964, pp. 143-144; Newsweek, November 16, 1964, p. 92.

Critical Reputation:

    Robert Lowell (1917-), one of America's most
distinguished poets, was born in Boston of an old New
England family, studied in private schools, then at Harvard
and finally at Kenyon College, where he received the A.B.
in 1940. During World War II, Lowell, a conscientious ob-
jector, refused the draft and served a prison term. In 1947
he won a Pulitzer Prize for his volume of poems Lord
Weary's Castle. His newer poems are collected in For the
Union Dead (1964) and in Near the Ocean (1967). A critical
biography is Hugh Stepler's Robert Lowell: The First Twenty
Years, 1961. For a recent study, see Jerome Mazzaro's
The Poetic Themes of Robert Lowell, 1965. For discussions
of The Old Glory, consult Robert Brustein's Seasons of Discontent, 1965, pp. 252-259; Harold Clurman's The Naked
Image: Observations on the Modern Theatre, 1966, pp. 94-
97; and Baruch Hochman's "Robert Lowell's The Old Glory,"
Tulane Drama Review, XI (Summer 1967), 127-138.

ONE WORLD AT A TIME

Characters:

Ebon Ingersoll	Eva Ingersoll
Bob Ingersoll	Judge Palmer
Deacon Ripley	Vestryman Black
Deacon Aldrich	Vestryman Stanhope
Deacon Lamb	Whitehead
The Rev. John Ingersoll	C. J.

Act I:

When the Ingersoll brothers, Ebon and Bob, start practicing law in 1857 in Peoria, Illinois, trouble is inevitable. Ebon tries to be tolerant when Bob, a militant and articulate atheist, loses their first clients, deacons from the Baptist church. His patience, however, is sorely tried when Bob refuses to mute his opinions before their father, a retired minister of the gospel. Only during Ebon's successful campaign for the U.S. Congress does Bob curtail his heretical speeches.

Act II:

Three years later, Bob, now married to a charming freethinker, has political hopes himself. His success in the governor's race is assured when the influential Judge Parker promises his support if Bob will conceal his controversial views, but this Bob refuses to do. Embittered, he launches a career as an agnostic preacher, a vocation which his father, from his deathbed, begs him to repudiate.

Act III:

Twelve years later, Bob has become a successful lecturer in New York, but his position threatens Ebon's political career. Ebon accuses Bob of sacrificing everything--their father's happiness, his own political career, and now Ebon's--to his fanatical desire to speak his mind. Bob goes to his lecture that evening with his brother's rebuke in his ears. Furthermore, his life has been threatened by a crank who vows to shoot him that night if he disparages the God of his fathers. Bob impulsively discards his prepared speech and addresses the would-be assassin in the audience, eloquently defending the right to think and express ideas freely. As he concludes, he spreads his arms and in-

vites the killer to end a life dedicated to the pursuit of
truth.   No shot is fired.

Theatre History:

One World at a Time was presented by the Burlington
Players, May 4 through 7, 1966.   After the Iowa performance, Stockton submitted the first act to a national one-act
contest and it won.   Unfortunately, the play has not yet received a professional production.

Critical Reputation:

Richard Stockton (1932-   ), free-lance stage, television, and radio dramatist, received his B.A. from Akron
University and did graduate work in playwriting at U.C.L.A.,
where he had seven plays produced.   After receiving the
M.A. in 1958, he was appointed Graduate Fellow in Playwriting at the State University of Ohio.   At one time, Stockton held more awards for playwriting than anyone else in the
country, but his work has never been professionally produced
in New York.   He is now a professional speechwriter, although he has not given up writing.   He has had three children's musicals produced and hopes to have an historical
play premiered at the Abbey Theatre in Dublin.

The Theatre Season of

1965-1966

The Pulitzer Prize was withheld this season. Both
the Circle and the Tony went to the foreign import Marat /
Sade by Peter Weiss. Ronald Ribman won the Obie with his
play Journey of the Fifth Horse, a dramatization of Ivan
Turgenev's Diary of a Superfluous Man. Also appearing this
season were: Generation, Hogan's Goat, Cactus Flower and
The Lion in Winter.

JOURNEY OF THE FIFTH HORSE

Characters:

Terentievna
Zoditch
Sergey
Rubin (also Capt. Ivan
   Narvinsky)
Miss Grubov (also
   Elizaveta Ozhogin)
Pandalevski (also
   Bizmionkov)
Katerine Prolomnaya

Nikolai Alexeevitch
   Chulkaturin
Dr. Korvin
Lawyer Lavinov
Feathers (also Volbrina)
Kirilla Matveich Ozhogin
Anna Nikitishna Ozhogin
Gregory
Tenia
Lt. Zimin
Officers

Act I:

At the Grubov Publishing House on the day of the
owner's funeral, an old woman tries to interest Zoditch, a
reader, in a diary written by her late master, Nikolai Chulkaturin, on his deathbed. Zoditch, however, is more interested in currying the favor of Miss Grubov, now the owner of the firm. Others have the same idea, and Zoditch, in
spite of his obsequious behavior, is shouldered aside. Later,
in his dingy apartment, he has a vision of Pandalevski, a
printer in tne Grubov firm, who leeringly tells Zoditch that

187

Miss Grubov has encouraged his attentions and wishes to marry him. Zoditch then imagines himself making love to Miss Grubov until Rubin, another of the office toadies, displaces him in the bed.

At this point, Zoditch begins to read the diary. The writer, a kind and sensitive man, died believing himself a "superfluous man, " isolated from his fellows and unsuccessful in every venture. He describes himself as a fifth horse tied to a four-in-hand--no good to the other horses and attached to the carriage in such a way as to be in almost constant pain. Zoditch, unable to see the nobility of Chulkaturin's character, finds him unbearably sentimental, but as the diarist recounts his thwarted courtship with Liza, a girl who is seduced and abandoned by a cavalry officer, Zoditch begins to see the characters in the story as projections of people he knows: Liza becomes Miss Grubov; her father is Mr. Grubov; the Army officer is Rubin; the man who marries Liza is Pandalevski.

Act II:

Chulkaturin risks his life in a duel with the captain and then offers to marry Liza, who is now pregnant. Liza jilts him, however, and marries Bizmionkov, an old family friend. Paralleling Chulkaturin's rejection is Zoditch's rejection by his tyrannical landlady who Zoditch fancied was in love with him. When he approaches her, however, she rudely refuses his offer and even raises his rent. Later, upon reading of Chulkaturin's humiliation at the hands of Liza, Zoditch cries out "Liar! I am the one that is loved! That is the ending, " and throws the manuscript away.

Theatre History and Popular Response:

Journey of the Fifth Horse, produced by the American Place Theatre at St. Clement's Church, opened April 31, 1966, and ran for eleven performances. Most of the reviews were favorable. Although some of the critics complained that the play's structure was overelaborate and clumsy, most expressed admiration for Ribman's innovative use of the Turgenev materials. For representative reviews, see: Commonweal, May 27, 1966, p. 283; Nation, May 30, 1966, p. 661; New Republic, May 7, 1966, p. 31; New Yorker, April 30, 1966, p. 79.

Critical Reputation:

Ronald Ribman (1932-   ) was born in New York City. He studied at the University of Pittsburgh, from which he received the B.B.A. (1954), the M. Litt. (1958), and the Ph.D. (1962). He taught English in college for a time, then made his theatre debut with Harry, Noon and Night (1965). Some of his recent plays are Ceremony of Innocence (1967), The Final War of Olly Winter (1967), and The Inheritors (1969). For a useful discussion of Ribman's work, including Journey of the Fifth Horse, see Martin Gottfried's A Theatre Divided, 1967, pp. 74-75; and Gerald Weales' The Jumping-Off Place, 1969, pp. 229-234.

The Theatre Season of

1966-1967

The Pulitzer Prize went this season to Edward Albee's
A Delicate Balance. A British play, The Homecoming, by
Harold Pinter, captured both the Circle and the Tony Award.
No Obie was awarded. Also running were: America Hurrah,
You Know I Can't Hear You When The Water's Running,
Don't Drink the Water, The Star-Spangled Girl, MacBird!
and The Deer Park.

A DELICATE BALANCE

Characters:

Agnes	Julia
Tobias	Harry
Claire	Edna

Act I:

Tobias, a retired businessman; Agnes, his articulate,
acerbic wife; and Claire, Agnes' alcoholic younger sister,
live together in a precariously balanced menage. This balance is disturbed when Harry and Edna, long time friends
of Tobias and Agnes, arrive and announce that some name-
less terror has seized them. In the name of friendship,
Agnes and Tobias take them in.

Act II:

Following the collapse of her fourth marriage, Agnes
and Tobias' daughter Julia comes home. When she finds
Harry and Edna installed in her bedroom, she is resentful,
especially as it appears they intend to stay indefinitely. One
night Julia's hostility surfaces and she hysterically brandishes
a pistol at the guests and orders Tobias to throw them out.
Edna calmly slaps her, then asserts that she and Harry have

as much right to be in the house as Julia does.

Act III:

In desperation, Tobias appeals to Agnes to help him decide what to do about Harry and Edna, but she declines, reminding Tobias that at every crisis in their lives he has made the choices (or failed to make them) while she accepted the results and tried to hold the family together. Finally, in an hysterical outburst, Tobias tells Harry that he and Edna must stay, even though he and Agnes do not really want them for fear they will infect them with their terror and upset the balance of their accommodations. Harry and Edna, now realizing that they would not have taken in Tobias and Agnes under similar circumstances, prepare to leave. Numb with embarrassment, the couples bid each other good-bye. Tobias senses that he has failed somehow, but Agnes at once begins to pat her little family back into shape.

Theatre History and Popular Response:

A Delicate Balance opened at the Martin Beck Theatre on September 22, 1966, and ran for 132 performances. The critics disagreed as to the merits of the play, but several considered it Albee's best work so far, a more mature and less sensational play than Who's Afraid of Virginia Woolf? One called it "an engaging, almost ingratiating play...." Another praised its "brilliantly corroding and lacerating wit...." Albee accepted the Pulitzer Prize somewhat reluctantly, still piqued because Virginia Woolf had been passed over. He pronounced the Pulitzer Prize "an honor in decline," and said he might use the money to establish a fund to train responsible drama critics. For representative reviews of the play, see: Commonweal, October 14, 1966, pp. 55-56; Nation, October 10, 1966, pp. 361-363; New Republic, October 8, 1966, pp. 35-36; Reporter, October 20, 1966, pp. 52-53.

Critical Reputation:

For a brief introduction to Albee's life and work, see the entry for 1962-1963. Discussions of A Delicate Balance can be found in John Gassner's Dramatic Soundings, 1968, pp. 603-607; and in Gerald Weales' The Jumping-Off Place, 1969, pp. 24-53. Two useful critical articles are C. W. E.

Bigsby's "Tragedy of Madness: An Analysis of Edward Albee's A Delicate Balance," Contemporary Literature, IX
(April 13, 1968), 223-234; and John Simon's "Theatre Chronicle," Hudson Review, XIX (1966-1967), 627-629. Michael
Rutenberg's book Edward Albee: Playwright in Protest,
1969, contains an analysis of the play.

The Theatre Season of

1967-1968

In this lean year for prizes, neither the Pulitzer nor
the Circle nor the Tony was awarded. The Obie went to
Rosencrantz and Guildenstern Are Dead by the British playwright Tom Stoppard.

The Theatre Season of

1968-1969

The Great White Hope, Howard Sackler's play based
on the career of Jack Johnson, the Negro boxer, swept the
field this season, winning the Pulitzer Prize, The Circle
Award, and the Tony Award. The Obie was not given. Also
competing for prizes this season were: Forty Carats, Ceremonies in Dark Old Men, We Bombed in New Haven, In the
Bar of a Tokyo Hotel, and Adaptation/Next.

THE GREAT WHITE HOPE

Characters:

Frank Brady	Blackface
Fred	Colonel Cox
Cap'n Dan	Deacon
Smitty	Donnelly
Goldie	Mrs. Bachman
Jack Jefferson	Cameron
Tick	Dixon
Ellie Bachman	Scipio
Clara	Mrs. Jefferson
Paster	Farlow
Rudy	Klossowski
Treacher	Pop Weaver
Eubanks	Ragosy
Sir William Griswold	Negro
Coates	Peco
Mrs. Kimball	El Jefe
Inspector Wainwright	A Young Federal Agent
Bratby	The Kid

Act I:

When Jack Jefferson, a young Negro boxer, becomes
Heavyweight Champion of the world, his troubles begin.

Many whites in Chicago, resentful of the black man's victory and outraged because he has a white mistress, pressure the District Attorney to find a criminal charge against him. The District Attorney knows that Jack has broken no laws, but in desperation, he questions Ellie, Jack's girl. He can find nothing illegal in their relationship, but later, when Jack and Ellie go to a vacation cottage in Wisconsin, federal agents arrest him for violation of the Mann Act. Jack, sentenced to three years in prison, escapes and goes to England.

Act II:

Jack and Ellie wander from London to Paris to Berlin, never really welcome anywhere. Jack, now moody and irritable, fights fifth-rate boxers and quarrels with Ellie to pass the time. Meanwhile, law enforcement officers in the U.S., eager for the defeat of the black champion, offer to reduce Jack's sentence to six months if he will agree to a fixed match. Jack refuses. Finally, he and Ellie are reduced to playing Uncle Tom and Little Eva to jeering audiences in a Belgrade cabaret. Even though his life as World Champion is miserable, he cannot relinquish the title until someone beats him in a fair fight.

Act III:

Jack and Ellie drift to Mexico where they quarrel savagely. Finally, Jack orders Ellie to leave him. After she goes, federal agents from the U.S. arrive and offer Jack a suspended sentence in exchange for a fixed match. Jack refuses at first, but when he learns that Ellie has killed herself, he surrenders. The fight, which takes place in Havana, goes to ten rounds with Jack the winner. The promoters, fearing that Jack has double-crossed them, send word reminding him of the deal. Still Jack refuses to give up. Finally, however, his opponent's punches begin to connect, and Jack loses. Whether he is beaten fairly or simply gives up is left open to question.

Theatre History and Popular Response:

The Great White Hope had its premiere at Washington's Arena Stage, then opened on Broadway at the Alvin Theatre on October 3, 1968, and ran for 556 performances. The critics took note of the play's faulty structure and weaknesses in characterization, but they praised its "epic scope"

and sheer dramatic power.   For representative reviews,
see: Nation, January 15, 1968, pp. 48-50; New Republic,
October 26, 1968, p. 36; New Yorker, October 12, 1968,
p. 103; Time, October 11, 1968, p. 73.

Critical Reputation:

    Howard Sackler (1929-) was born in New York City
and studied at Brooklyn College (B.A. 1950).   He has written extensively for television and movies, has directed dramatic recordings, and is the author of several plays, some
of which have been produced abroad and some in the regional
theatres of this country.   He is also a poet whose work has
appeared in several prestigious journals.   For a discussion
of The Great White Hope, see Julius Novick's Beyond Broadway: The Quest for a Permanent Theatre, 1968, pp. 48-50.
See also Andrew Sarris's discussion of the play and the re-
sulting motion picture in The Village Voice, October 29,
1970, p. 59, and November 5, 1970, p. 53 ff.

The Theatre Season of

1969-1970

The Pulitzer Prize went this season to Charles Gordone for his play No Place To Be Somebody. The Drama Critics gave the Circle Award to The Effects of Gamma Rays on Man-in-the-Moon Marigolds by Paul Zindel. (The Pulitzer Committee considered Marigolds a play of the 1970-1971 season and selected it a year after it won the Circle.) Marigolds also tied with Megan Terry's Approaching Simone for the Obie. The Tony went to Borstal Boy, Frank McMahon's adaptation of a book by the Irishman Brendan Behan. Also running were: Indians, Butterflies Are Free, Last of the Red Hot Lovers and Child's Play.

NO PLACE TO BE SOMEBODY

Characters:

Gabe Gabriel	Cora Beasely
Shanty Mulligan	Melvin Smeltz
Johnny Williams	Mary Lou Bolton
Dee Jacobson	Ellen
Evie Ames	Sweets Crane
Mike Maffucci	Sergeant Cappaletti
Truck Driver	Harry
Judge Bolton	Louie
Machine Dog	

Act I:

Johnny Williams' West Village saloon is the gathering place for a group of misfits, both black and white. Gabe Gabriel, a fair-skinned Negro who announces in the opening moments that he is the author of the play, is unable to make a living as an actor because he does not look Negroid enough. Shanty Mulligan, a white boy with a Negro's soul, wants to be a drummer but fears that Cora, his black mistress, will

196

sap his talent by reinforcing his whiteness. Johnny, a black, dreams of making big money as a racketeer, but his operations are limited to pimping and petty crimes because the Mafia severely curtails his activities. Frustrated and bitter, Johnny awaits the return of Sweets Crane, his mentor and partner, now serving a prison sentence. Johnny, who assumed Sweets would help him break into the rackets, is dismayed to learn that Sweets has shaken off "Charlie fever," embraced religion and reformed.

Act II:

Johnny continues to try to enlist Sweets' help, but the old man, now fatally ill, refuses and pleads with Johnny to give up crime. Instead, Johnny decides to take on the Mafia alone. Meanwhile, he has become involved with a white girl, Mary Lou Bolton, a naive civil rights activist, whose father, now a judge, once defended Pete Zeroni, one of the mobsters Johnny is fighting.

Act III:

When Dee, Johnny's pathetic white mistress, learns about Mary Lou and Johnny, she kills herself. Mary Lou, now completely smitten by Johnny, steals papers from her father's files implicating Zeroni in a murder. Gabe tells the girl that Johnny wants to use the information to blackmail his way into the rackets, a fact Johnny freely admits. When Johnny learns that the Judge intends to sacrifice his daughter (who has been picked up for soliciting for Johnny) to save himself, he gives back the papers. Later, two mobsters come to kill Johnny, but he and Sweets kill them. Sweets, dying from the exertion, makes Johnny promise to reform, but after he dies, Johnny admits to Gabe that he has no intention of changing. Gabe, in a rage, kills him. In the last scene, Machine Dog, a dream figure who had earlier appeared to Johnny and inducted him into a militant black organization, appears and accuses the oppressors of the black man. Then Gabe, dressed as a woman in mourning, addresses the audience, saying that he mourns "the death of a people dying into a new life."

Theatre History and Popular Response:

No Place to Be Somebody was first produced at the New York Shakespeare Festival Public Theatre. The play

opened on May 4, 1969, and ran for 250 performances. It
was later given 16 performances at the ANTA Theatre beginning on December 30, 1969. Subsequently remounted in
an off-Broadway revival, the play was still running when
Gordone received the Pulitzer Prize. Critical reaction was
mixed. Some reviewers complained of the play's episodic
structure and melodramatic ending, but most also praised
the play for being beyond "the cliches of racial relations."
One critic pronounced Gordone "the most astonishing new
American playwright to come along since Edward Albee."
For representative reviews, see: America, September 6,
1969, p. 145; Nation, May 19, 1969, p. 644; New Yorker,
May 17, 1969, p. 112; Time, May 16, 1969, pp. 85-86.

Critical Reputation:

        Charles Gordone (1925-   ), the first black man to
win the Pulitzer Prize for Drama, was born at Elkhart,
Indiana, and attended public schools. He attended U.C.L.A.,
but left to join the Army. Later he earned a degree in
drama from Los Angeles State College. He has been a
carnival and circus performer, a teacher of elocution, an
actor, a director, and associate producer of a motion picture.
No Place To Be Somebody is his first produced play, and as
yet, it has attracted little serious scholarly attention. For
a brief discussion of his career, see Ebony, July, 1970, pp.
29-37.

THE EFFECT OF GAMMA RAYS
ON MAN-IN-THE-MOON MARIGOLDS

Characters:

        Tillie   Nanny
        Beatrice   Janice Vickery
        Ruth

Act I:

        Beatrice Hunsdorfer, who pronounces her life a com-
plete zero, lives with her two daughters in a shabby building
that was once her father's vegetable shop. One daughter,
Ruth, has had a nervous collapse and is subject to convul-
sions. Tillie, the younger, is bright, poetic, sensitive, and
an outstanding student in science, but Beatrice takes little

interest in her talents and often keeps her home from school
to do household chores. Completing the menage is Nanny,
an ancient and senile woman whom Beatrice boards for $50
a month. Frustrated and bitter about the way her life has
turned out, Beatrice constantly regales her daughters with
stories of her brilliance and popularity at school. She
claims, in fact, that had she not married the wrong man,
she would now be rich and famous. When she learns that
Tillie's science project (growing marigolds from seeds exposed to gamma rays) has been selected for the finals of the
science fair, Beatrice reacts violently, declaring that she
will not go to the contest because she has nothing to wear
and people will laugh at her.

Act II:

On the night of the judging, Beatrice, secretly proud
of Tillie's achievement, prepares to attend the contest.
Ruth, in a fit of pique at having to stay home with Nanny,
tells her mother what she overheard from a teacher, namely,
that everyone in Beatrice's high school class called her
"Betty the Loon" behind her back. Beatrice refuses to
leave the house and while the girls are out, she drinks
heavily, then chloroforms Tillie's pet rabbit. Tillie returns
victorious, but her happiness is cut short when Ruth, at the
sight of the dead pet, has a violent convulsion. Beatrice,
stricken by what she has done, weakly tells Tillie, "I hate
the world." Tillie, mature beyond her years, understands.

Theatre History and Popular Response:

The Effect of Gamma Rays on Man-in-the-Moon Marigolds was originally produced in 1964 at the Alley Theatre in
Houston, Texas. The play's New York run began on April 7,
1970, at the Mercer-O'Casey Theatre. It was still running
at this writing. Enthusiastically received by reviewers, the
play was called "a great human drama" and Zindel "one of
our most promising new writers." Several of the critics
compared Zindel to Tennessee Williams and called the play
the finest of its kind since The Glass Menagerie. For representative reviews, see: Life, July 4, 1970, pp. 8-9; Nation, April 20, 1970, p. 476; New Yorker, April 18, 1970,
p. 82; Saturday Review, May 2, 1970, p. 12.

Critical Reputation:

  Paul Zindel (1936-) was born at Staten Island and
attended Wagner College. He taught chemistry in high
school for a time, then turned his attention to full time
writing. Zindel is both a novelist and a playwright. Two
of his novels, The Pigman and My Darling, My Hamburger,
were selected as "Outstanding Books of the Year" by the
New York Times. Both, together with a third, I Never
Loved Your Mind, are being made into motion pictures.
Zindel has also served as Playwright-in-Residence at the
Alley Theatre in Houston, where Marigolds had its debut.

APPROACHING SIMONE

  Approaching Simone, as yet unpublished and known to
me only through reviews, is about Simone Weil, the French
philosopher and mystic. The play, which presents a series
of vignettes which record the journey of a soul, begins in
1914 when Miss Weil is a precocious child of five, progresses through her student days, shows her career as a
lycée teacher and then a factory worker, her entrance into
radical politics when she joins the Loyalists in Spain, her
mystical conversion to Christianity, and finally, her death
in 1943 in a London sanatorium after she refuses to eat
more than the starvation rations provided those in the
French Resistance Movement.

Theatre History and Popular Response:

  Miss Terry wrote Approaching Simone for the cen-
tennial of Boston University, and the play was first produced
by that school's Division of Theatre Arts, then brought to
the LaMama Experimental Theatre Club in New York. It
got a complimentary review in the New York Times, and the
critic pronounced the play "a rare theatrical event...."
Another called it "one of the most powerful and engrossing
pieces of theatre to be seen in New York this season." For
representative reviews, see: America, June 6, 1970, p.
612; and Newsweek, March 16, 1970, p. 64.

Critical Reputation:

  Information about Miss Terry is difficult to come by.

Gerald Weales complains, for example, that she and her publisher are reluctant to supply even the dates of her plays. Her agent, however, supplied the following data for this guide.

Megan Terry was born in Seattle, Washington. She graduated from the University of Washington, and further, studied at the University of Alberta and the Banff School of Fine Arts and Yale. She began her training in the theatre in her early teens at the Seattle Repertory Playhouse. At 19, she re-organized the Cornish Players and toured the Northwest for two years. Miss Terry was a founding member of the Open Theatre, which has produced six of her plays: Eat at Joe's; Calm Down, Mother; Keep Tightly Closed in a Cool, Dry Place; Magic Realists; The Gloaming, Oh My Darling; and Viet Rock.

At present, Miss Terry conducts a permanent workshop in playmaking at Westbeth, lectures before college and theatre groups, and is a editorial advisor and script reader for Scripts magazine.

The Theatre Season of

1970-1971

The Pulitzer Committee considered last year's Circle
and Obie winner, Paul Zindel's The Effects of Gamma Rays
on Man-in-the-Moon Marigolds, a play of the 1970-1971 season and awarded it the Pulitzer Prize. Both the Circle and
the Obie went to John Guare's zany farce The House of Blue
Leaves. Sleuth, the British thriller by Anthony Shaffer,
won the Tony. Also running were: Steambath, The Trial of
the Catonsville Nine, and The Gingerbread Lady.

THE HOUSE OF BLUE LEAVES

Characters:

Artie Shaughnessy   The Head Nun
Ronnie Shaughnessy   The Second Nun
Bunny Flingus   The Little Nun
Bananas Shaughnessy   The M.P.
Corinna Stroller   The White Man
Billy Einhorn

Prologue:

On the stage of the El Dorado Bar and Grill, a bar
where amateurs perform their works, a nervous Artie Shaughnessy, zookeeper and aspiring songwriter, sings his songs to
an unappreciative and inattentive audience. The management
of the bar will not even give him the blue spotlight he re-
quested.

Act I:

On the day of the Pope's visit to New York, Artie
finally decides to take his destiny in his hands. With the
encouragement of his mistress, Bunny Flingus, he makes up
his mind to have his mad wife, Bananas, committed to a

202

mental institution that he calls The House of Blue Leaves
because he saw on its grounds a tree full of blue birds.
Like the birds, Artie is eager to fly away with Bunny to
California where his childhood friend, Billy Einhorn, now a
famous movie magnate, has promised to help him begin his
career as a songwriter. After firming up his arrangements
with Billy on the telephone, Artie takes Bunny and Bananas
out to see the Pope's parade.

Act II:

Meanwhile, Artie's son Ronnie, whose life was
wrecked when Billy failed to select him to play Huckleberry
Finn, is A.W.O.L. from Fort Dix. He plans to gain the
notoriety he craves by blowing up the Pope with a homemade
bomb. When Artie and the two women return, they are
joined by Billy's mistress, Corinna Stroller, and three nuns
who ask to come in and watch the Pope on television. Ronnie, still smoldering with resentment toward Billy, gives
Corinna the package with the bomb. She and two of the
three nuns die in the explosion which no one realizes Ronnie
has caused.

Later that night, when Billy comes to claim Corinna's
body, he meets Bunny, suddenly forgets his grief, and persuades her to run away with him. He also calls a friend at
the Pentagon and gets Ronnie out of the brig and reassigned,
ironically, to duty in Rome. Artie, his dream now a sham-
ble, is left alone with Bananas, whom he strangles as the
stage slowly fills with falling blue leaves. As the play ends,
Artie steps downstage into a blue spotlight, introduces himself to the audience, and begins to sing his songs.

Theatre History and Popular Response:

The House of Blue Leaves opened its long run on
February 10, 1971, at the Truck and Warehouse Theatre.
Generally, the notices were favorable. Critics hailed Guare
as an impressive talent, "one who certainly can't be ig-
nored." They called the play "brilliant," "original," and
"very funny." One pronounced it "the most striking new
American play of the season." A few, however, complained
that the play was muddled, and that the second act was "one
long turn for the worse." For representative reviews, see:
Nation, March 1, 1971, pp. 285-186; New Yorker, February
20, 1971, p. 90; Saturday Review, March 20, 1971, p. 10.

<u>Critical Reputation</u>:

     John Guare (1938-), was born in Manhattan but grew up in Queens where he attended Catholic schools. He graduated from Georgetown University in 1961, then took the M.A. in English at Yale. His one-act play <u>Muzeeka</u> (1968), with which he made his debut off-off Broadway, won him an Obie for distinguished playwriting. The following year, his play <u>Cop-Out</u> was produced on Broadway. It ran for only a week, but the Variety critics' poll voted him the most promising playwright of the year. A recent achievement is his contribution to the successful musical <u>Two Gentlemen of Verona</u>, for which he helped adapt the book and to which he contributed the lyrics. No doubt Guare's work will attract serious critical attention, but as of this writing, no studies of his plays have appeared.

INDEX